ESCAPING THE
MATRIX

Setting Your Mind Free
to Experience Real Life in Christ

Gregory A. Boyd
and
Al Larson

BakerBooks
Grand Rapids, Michigan

© 2005 by Gregory A. Boyd and Al Larson

Published by Baker Books
a division of Baker Publishing Group
P.O. Box 6287, Grand Rapids, MI 49516-6287
www.bakerbooks.com

Third printing, June 2006

Printed in the United States of America

Library of Congress Cataloging-in-Publication Data
Boyd, Gregory A., 1957–
    Escaping the matrix : setting your mind free to experience real life in
  Christ / Gregory A. Boyd and Al Larson.
        p.   cm.
    Includes bibliographical references.
    ISBN 10: 0-8010-6533-X
    ISBN 978-0-8010-6533-0
    1. Matrix (Motion picture) 2. Motion pictures—Religious aspects—
  Christianity. I. Larson, Al, 1948– II. Title.
  PN1997.M395B69 2005
  791.43'72—dc22   2004026953

Contents

Introduction

The Bible, Neuroscience, and the Matrix

Most of her life Mary had been depressed. She didn't know why and didn't know how to get out of it. She loved Jesus, had a near ideal upbringing, and went to church regularly. She had been in and out of therapy most of her life, took antidepression medications, and had been prayed for repeatedly—including several attempted exorcisms. Yet Mary remained depressed. A not-quite-professional term Mary used to describe her condition was that she was "stuck."

In one way or another, most of us are stuck. You may be stuck in a rage you can't control or an inability to get angry when you should. You may be stuck in a fear of intimate relationships or an inability to avoid them, even when they're inappropriate. You may be stuck in an inability to get excited about much of anything or in a virtual addiction to excitement. You may be stuck in a pattern of lustful thoughts or in an inability to become sexually aroused toward your spouse. You may have a compulsion to shop, an inferiority or superiority complex, a judgmental attitude you can't shut off, a persistent feeling of guilt, an ongoing and pervasive anxiety, a tendency toward self-hatred, or an addiction to pornography. All are evidence of being stuck.

Now, no one likes to be stuck. It's always life-inhibiting, usually painful, and often downright destructive. In all likelihood you've tried hard to get unstuck. Yet, despite all the self-help techniques you've tried, the willpower you've exerted, the resolutions you've made, and the prayers you've prayed, you remain the same.

What's particularly frustrating and puzzling about this for believers is that Scripture seems to promise us that things would be very different. Aren't we supposed to be "more than conquerors" (Rom. 8:37)? Aren't we supposed to be "new creations" in Christ (2 Cor. 5:17)? Aren't we supposed to experience abundant life and be filled with the love, joy, peace, and power of God himself (e.g., John 10:10; Phil. 4:18; 1 Thess. 1:6; 2 Tim. 1:7)?

What is the problem?

Oddly enough, we submit that a most profound clue to an answer to this question is found in the blockbuster movie *The Matrix*.[1] Few movies have captured the imagination of people like *The Matrix*, along with its two sequels, *The Matrix Reloaded* and *The Matrix Revolutions*. These three movies—but especially the first one—have inspired a remarkable amount of philosophical and religious discussion. Much has been said about the ingenious way in which the Wachowski brothers weave together Christian, Gnostic, Buddhist, and ancient Greek ideas, myths, and symbols. And a good deal has been written on the assortment of intriguing philosophical and psychological questions raised by these movies. Are humans free or determined? What is the nature of reality? Is technology a friend or a foe?

Yet, what is in our minds the most profound aspect of the *Matrix* movies has not been addressed. It concerns the basic metaphor of the Matrix itself.

In the movie *The Matrix*, humanity is enslaved by an artificial intelligence we ourselves created. Humans are kept in pods while their bodies are used as energy sources to support the machinery of artificial intelligence. To keep us enslaved, the artificial intelligence creates a massive, interactive, virtual reality for humans. And by meticulously controlling the neurons in our brains, the artificial intelligence manages to deceive us into thinking this virtual world is the real world. Though we are in fact enslaved in cocoonlike pods, we experience ourselves and our world just as we do now. Everything seems normal. Everything feels real.

The neurologically controlled virtual reality that keeps us imprisoned is the Matrix.

The most profound aspect of *The Matrix* and its sequels is the powerful way in which the Matrix metaphor fuses biblical truth with the findings of neuroscience. On the one hand, the metaphor illustrates the biblical concept of a "pattern of this world" (Rom. 12:2) that has an evil, cosmic force—a "god of this age" (Satan)—as its architect (2 Cor. 4:4; see also Eph. 2:2; 1 John 5:19). On the other hand, the metaphor brilliantly illustrates the neurological truth that our entire experience of reality is rooted in the electrical-chemical firings in our brains.

At one point Neo asks Morpheus if his experience in the Matrix is "real." Morpheus responds, "What is real? How do you define real? If you're talking about what you can feel, what you can smell, what you can taste and see, then real is simply electrical signals interpreted by your brain."

The plausibility and profundity of the Matrix concept resides in the fact that Morpheus was speaking accurately to Neo. The fact is our entire experience of ourselves and the world is indeed a *neurologically generated construct*—a matrix. Everything we experience is at base a network of neurons in our brains firing on one another in patterned ways. Everything you experience is in fact "electrical signals interpreted by your brain."

The book you're holding and the words you're reading right now, the smell of your coffee nearby, the feeling of the weight of your body on the chair in which you're sitting, the room you're in, the sounds you're hearing, your memory of yesterday, and your thoughts about tomorrow—all are electrical-chemical reactions in your brain. Based on information stored in neurons, your brain automatically attaches meaning to every distinct aspect of this electrical-chemical activity. It interprets one pattern of electrical signals (called a "neural-net") as a book, another as the smell of coffee, another as a chair, and another as a thought about tomorrow. And it interprets each of these activated neurological networks as conveying "the real world."

Yet, it's just possible that your interpretation of your electrical signals is wrong—and herein lies the neurological plausibility of the premise of the *Matrix* movies. It's just possible that at times something other than "reality" is stimulating your neurons to fire the way they do. It's just possible that what's activating the brain's neural-nets is not the "outside world" at all but a sinister artificial intelligence—or an evil, cosmic force.

The central thesis of this book is that, from a biblical and neurological perspective, the premise of the *Matrix* movies is not only possible, but to a significant degree *it's true*! No, we're not going to suggest that our sense of the physical world around us is illusory. You *really are* reading a book right now. But we are going to show that much of what we automatically interpret as "real" is not true. A "god of this age" (2 Cor. 4:4) has seized the world and created a deceptive pattern, a "dream world"—a Matrix—that holds us in bondage. We are to a large degree conformed to "the pattern of this world" instead of to the truth of who we are in Christ (Rom. 12:2). We find ourselves imprisoned in patterns of electrical signals that we interpret as real but that are not true. Our experience of reality is to this extent aligned with the schemes of an evil Architect (Satan) rather than God. Hence, we do not experience ourselves as we truly are in Christ.

This, we shall show, is the most fundamental reason why Mary (whose story we will tell) remained stuck in her depression and why each of us remains stuck in one way or another. We are caught in the Matrix.

In *The Matrix*, Neo is offered a red pill that opens his mind to the bondage of the Matrix world and frees him to see and experience truth. It is our prayer that God will use this book as a sort of "red pill" for its readers. "Taking the red pill" involves waking up to our neurologically controlled bondage, understanding how the Matrix operates, and learning how to wage war within the Matrix in ways that can set one free. Hence, part 1 of this book ("What Is the Matrix?") explores how the Matrix operates, while part 2 ("Escaping the Matrix") discusses practical ways of being set free.

It is our prayer that this book will help you be no longer conformed to the Matrix of this world but rather transformed by the renewing of your mind (Rom. 12:2). It is our prayer that this book will be used to open "the eyes of your heart" so you may "know the hope to which [God] has called you, the riches of his glorious inheritance to the saints," by experiencing firsthand his "incomparably great power for us who believe" (Eph. 1:18–19). It is our hope and prayer that you will learn how to escape the Matrix and set your mind free to *experience real life in Jesus Christ*.

PART 1

What Is the Matrix?

I

A Splinter in Your Mind

Waking Up to the Matrix

MORPHEUS: You're here because you know something. What you know
you can't explain. But you feel it. You've felt it your entire
life. . . . There's something wrong with the world. You don't
know what it is, but it's there, like a splinter in your mind
driving you mad. It is this feeling that has brought you to me.
Do you know what I'm talking about?

NEO: The Matrix?

MORPHEUS: Do you want to know what *it* is?

———∞∞∞———

Do not conform any longer to the pattern of this world, but be
transformed by the renewing of your mind. Then you will be
able to test and approve what God's will is—his good, pleasing
and perfect will.

Romans 12:2

That Gnawing Sensation

Neo knew Morpheus was right. There was something wrong, something unreal, about the world he knew. There had to be more to life, and more to himself, than what he had thus far experienced. It gnawed at him like "a splinter in his mind."

Part of what makes *The Matrix* so intriguing is that on some level we all feel this way, at least sometimes. Something feels "off." The sensation takes many forms. It's that discomforting sense of futility that creeps up on you now and then. It's that unshakeable feeling that life is passing you by. It's that sense of disappointment we sometimes feel about ourselves. We're not all we want to be and know we should be. We're haunted by dreams long abandoned. It's that struggle with thoughts, feelings, and actions that seems to master us at times. It's that gnawing question that creeps into our consciousness now and then: is this all there is? For some odd reason, we thought there'd be more.

In one form or another, you feel a splinter in your mind.

We don't like splinters, of course, so most of us try to ignore it. Many try to suppress the emptiness and pain by staying insanely busy. We pour ourselves into daily chores—the kids, the cleaning, the job, the shopping. Some of us preoccupy ourselves with other people's lives—especially the lives of celebrities—trying to create the illusion that something worthy of our attention is going on somewhere. Some of us occupy ourselves with new things we hope to achieve, experience, or acquire. Some of us perpetually chase after new lovers, while others distract themselves with politics, sports, movies, upcoming vacations, or church work. When all else fails, some of us turn to alcohol or some other substance to numb the aching sensation.

But nothing pulls the splinter out. When the activity ceases, the adventure ends, the achievement is accomplished, or the game is over, the gnawing returns. Something is wrong. Something is missing. We know in the core of our being that we were created for more—much more. But what?

The Good News and a Splinter

As most of the readers of this book probably know, the gospel has a remedy for this gnawing sensation: you need Jesus! A truer statement could not be uttered.

The Bible teaches that we were created to be in fellowship with our Creator, who alone can fill our inner emptiness. Through Christ, we are told, we can experience "abundant life," life as God intended it, life lived out of a fullness of love, joy, and peace that only God can give. Indeed, in Christ we are given a new identity and made into a "new creation" (2 Cor. 5:17). Though we once were alienated from God and at war with God, in Christ we are forgiven, redeemed, reconciled to God, freed from all condemnation, and given eternal life as a free gift (see Rom. 3:24; 6:23; 1 Cor. 1:4; 2 Cor. 5:19; Eph. 4:32; 2 Tim. 1:1). We are indwelt with his Holy Spirit and have a River of Life longing to gush out of us (John 7:39). We are made to participate in the eternal, triune love of God that is his nature and are enabled to see in our minds the glory of God in the face of Jesus Christ (2 Cor. 3:14–4:6; 2 Peter 1:4). We have been set free from "the law of sin and death" and made to be God's own perfectly holy children (Rom. 8:2; Gal. 3:26; Heb. 10:14). As God's children we have "obtained an inheritance" that is "imperishable and undefiled" and that will therefore last forever (Eph. 1:11; 1 Peter 1:4 NASB).

The proclamation of the gospel could not be more glorious. *And yet . . .*

As wonderful as life in Christ is, doesn't the glory of these marvelous truths in a way exacerbate the gnawing sensation? If all this is true, then (let us be honest) why do our lives not reflect this, at least not with any degree of consistency?

The Bible says you're more than a conqueror in Christ (Rom. 8:37). Yet after twenty years of being a Christian, you still can't control your lust. Why is that?

The Bible says you've been filled with a Spirit-inspired, glorious joy that is beyond expression (1 Thess. 1:6; 1 Peter 1:8). Yet, though you've spiritually matured in many ways, you still struggle with depression. If what God says is true, how can that be?

The Bible says you can do all things through Christ who strengthens you (Phil. 4:13)—a truth you've believed for years. Yet you still back down from confrontation even though it allows others to walk all over you. Why is this?

For a decade you've believed the biblical truth that you've been given a spirit of power, love, and self-control (2 Tim. 1:7). Yet you still fear rejection and lose control with anger about as often as you did before you were a Christian. What aren't you getting?

For as long as you can remember, you've accepted the biblical truth that you are holy and redeemed in Christ (Gal. 3:13–14; Eph. 1:4). Yet you still sin in the same areas and maybe even to the same extent as you did before. And you likely live part of your life in shame because of it. What explains this?

You know that in Christ you are called and empowered to love all people, even your enemies. Yet you fear and avoid people who belong to a certain ethnic group. You know your lack of love—or it may be overt animosity—is not of God, yet you seem to have no power to change. Where's the transforming power of the gospel?

And though the Bible promises you abundant life (John 10:10), a truth you may have confessed for years, you still find yourself engaging in mundane distractions to stave off the aching splinter in your brain. You feel empty much, if not most, of the time. You perhaps sincerely *believe* what the Bible says is true, but you don't *experience* it as real most of the time. Hence, the truth doesn't fulfill you or transform you.

Yes, you know Jesus, but something is *still* wrong. And you're tired of it. You wish God were a genie who would just fold his arms, nod his head, and make it all better. No more emptiness. No more boredom. No more emotional pain. No more sin. No more wounds, weaknesses, and bondages. You wish it would all just magically disappear. Then you would know for sure God is real. Then you would be convinced God loves you and life is meaningful. But God doesn't do this.

You're tired and frustrated. A splinter remains in your brain.

Whatever the particular way your life mismatches biblical truth, you need to know this: *you are not alone*. Though Christians rarely admit such things out loud, this much is true of all of us. We accept the biblical truth, and our lives have undoubtedly changed somewhat because of it. But our lives still fall far short of the abundant life promised us in Christ. In fact, research shows that there is remarkably little difference between the attitudes and behaviors of Christians and non-Christians.[1] The way we experience ourselves and the world and the way we interact with others is basically the same as nonbelievers—despite the biblical truths we believe.

This is definitely not what the Bible promised. What's wrong?

A Couple Common—But Wrong—Answers

We might at this point expect a preacher to proclaim that our problem is that we are lazy and aren't working hard enough at costly discipleship. This may be true, but we don't think it's the basic problem for most people. It may very well be that you're utterly exhausted from trying hard to get your life to line up with what the Bible says is true about you.

Then again, we might expect a counselor to tell us that we need to be telling ourselves the truth more or perhaps that we should get into therapy. There is a great deal of truth in this perspective as well. But we don't for a moment believe this is the fundamental problem for most people either. Speaking biblical truths to ourselves helps a certain percentage of people if practiced persistently. We're all for it. But we're also aware that multitudes have earnestly practiced this and found it produced little change in their lives. Others have spent years in therapy with the same result. Simply knowing and even reciting true information doesn't seem to result in transformation—a point we shall explore later (chapter 3).

Finally, some address the gulf between God's Word and our lives by proclaiming that we are all just sinners and can't help ourselves. Hence, we shouldn't expect our lives to line up with God's Word. That's why we need grace.

Again, there is certainly some truth in this line of thinking. We are indeed all sinners who are perpetually in need of God's grace. Yet the Bible tells us we are *really* different when we submit to Christ. We are a "new creation" (2 Cor. 5:17). It's not just that God *sees us* as different, holy, spiritually empowered, and full of his life; we *really are this*. So the answer to our dilemma can't be to simply accept our sin, wounds, and misery. God wants us to experience *abundant life*!

If the problem isn't in our will or our knowledge, and if we aren't simply to accept ourselves as we are, what's the alternative?

What If . . . ?

> **TRINITY:** It's the question that drives us, Neo. It's the question that brought you here. You know the question just as I did.
>
> **NEO:** What is the Matrix?
>
> **TRINITY:** The answer is out there, Neo. It's looking for you.

What we're going to propose will sound as shocking to some as Morpheus's revelation about "the real world" was to Neo. However incredulous you may be, we're asking you not to put the book down just yet. Hang in there a little longer and we think you'll agree that, as difficult as our proposal may initially be to accept, it's actually deeply grounded in Scripture, confirmed by neuroscience, and, perhaps most importantly, *can and will be verified by you yourself.*

What if the real world not only mirrors the movie *The Matrix* in terms of the splinter we all have in our brains but also in *its explanation of this splinter*? What if we are in some sense *in a Matrix*? What if it's true that we allow the neurological activity in our brains to be significantly controlled by forces outside of ourselves? What if at least some of what we think is real is actually an illusion? And what if this is the explanation for why we don't consistently experience ourselves as being what Scripture says we truly are?

What if there really is a Matrix that holds us in bondage?

The Pattern of This World

If you trust the Bible, it shouldn't be that hard to believe in the existence of a Matrix. Consider what the apostle Paul taught: "Do not conform any longer to the pattern [*susche-*

matizo] of this world, but be transformed [*metamorphoo*] by the renewing of your mind. Then you will be able to test and approve what God's will is—his good, pleasing and perfect will" (Rom. 12:2).

Notice that the Greek word *suschematizo*, which is translated "pattern," could in fact be translated as "schema"—or yes, even "matrix." The Greek word *suschematizo* literally suggests the joining together (*su*) of matrixes or schemas (*schematizo*). Hence, the NIV appropriately translates the word "con [*with*] form . . . to the pattern."

Paul is teaching us that we are not to let the Matrix of the world control our minds, thoughts, and feelings. We are, rather, to be transformed—more literally, *metamorphosed*—out of it by the renewing of our minds. Our God-given destiny is for us to be transformed into the image of Christ (Rom. 8:29; 1 John 3:2), for this is who we *truly* are. The key to accomplishing this is to renew our minds away from the lies of the world's Matrix toward the truth of who we are in Christ. Morpheus explained to Neo:

> **Morpheus:** [The Matrix is] the world that has been pulled over your eyes to blind you from the truth.
>
> **Neo:** What truth?
>
> **Morpheus:** That you are a slave. Like everyone else you were born into bondage . . . [a] prison for your mind.

In biblical terms, "the god of this age has blinded the minds" of people to keep them from seeing and experiencing the truth (2 Cor. 4:4).

The Architect of the Matrix

The concept of "world" (*aion*) Paul uses in Romans 12:2 doesn't denote God's physical creation nor even the population of the earth. It rather denotes the present *world system* that is under the power of Satan and is hostile to God. It is an evil system (Gal. 1:4) that has its own wisdom (1 Cor. 2:6), its own standards (1 Cor. 3:18), its own earthly and spiritual rulers (1 Cor. 2:6, 8), and it is ultimately controlled by "the god of this age" (2 Cor. 4:4; see also 1 John 5:19). In the words of John Trench, it is a "floating mass of thoughts, opinions, maxims, speculations, hopes, impulses, aims, aspirations . . . which constitute a most real and effective power, being the moral or immoral atmosphere which at every moment of our lives we inhale."[2] *The world* is a structure of presuppositions and values that works at cross-purposes with the plans and values of the all-good Creator. Whereas the Creator's goal is to give abundant life to all who will receive it, the goal of this system, and of *the god of this world* who runs it, is to kill, steal, and destroy life wherever and whenever possible (John 10:10).

The architect and lord of this world system is none other than Satan. This is the one Paul refers to as "the god of this age," claiming he is the one blinding the minds of all unbelievers (2 Cor. 4:4). He also depicts Satan as "the ruler of the kingdom of the air" and says he is "the spirit who is now at work in those who are disobedient" (Eph. 2:2). Along similar lines, John teaches that "the whole world is under the control of the evil one" (1 John 5:19), while Jesus refers to Satan as "the prince of the world" (John 12:31; 14:30; 16:11). It's worth noting that the word translated "prince" in these passages (*archon*) denotes the highest ruling authority in a region. In terms of functional authority, Jesus is saying Satan is at the helm of the entire world system.

The remarkable authority the devil has over the world is also evidenced in his temptations of Jesus. Satan offers Jesus *all* the kingdoms of the world if only he will bow down and worship him. Satan claims that all these kingdoms belong to him and that he can give them to whomever he wants (Luke 4:6). Significantly enough, Jesus doesn't bat an eye at Satan's incredible claim! He concedes that Satan owns all this, but he refuses to worship Satan as a means of getting them back.[3]

Few Christians in the West take this teaching very seriously. If we *really* believe Satan controls the entire world and owns all the kingdoms of the world, do you think it would ever occur to us to ask, "Why do bad things happen to good people?" Would we not rather be amazed that there is any *goodness* left in the world at all? As it is, the majority of believers live their lives and think about their world as though Satan and his kingdom is an almost irrelevant consideration.

This naiveté works against us. Unless we wake up to the reality that the world is saturated by lies and that these lies affect us, we will not be motivated or empowered to replace the lies with truth and be set free. In fact, we won't likely recognize many of the lies as being lies at all! This is why Paul teaches us that "we are not to be ignorant of [Satan's] designs" (2 Cor. 2:11 NASB).

The most fundamental aspect of Satan's cosmic design, and the most basic strategy he uses to steal the abundant life God wants to give us, is deception. Jesus said that "there is no truth in him" and that "when he lies, he speaks his native language, for he is a liar and the father of lies" (John 8:44). This is how Satan co-opts humans into his rebellion against God in the first place. He paints a false picture of God as unloving, a false picture of humans as needing to acquire life on their own, and a false picture of disobedience as something that will give us life rather than destroy it (Gen. 3:1–5).

The primary power Satan has over the world is the power of lies. He is the cosmic deceiver who "leads the whole world astray" (Rev. 12:9; 13:14; 20:3, 8). Through deception he influences us to experience the unreal as real, evil as good, and death as life. Jesus teaches us that when we know the truth we are set free (John 8:32). But the reverse is also true. When we believe a lie we are, to that degree, in bondage. By means of deception Satan attempts to lead our minds astray and take us captive, just as he did Adam and Eve (2 Cor. 11:3; see also 2 Tim. 2:24–26).

The One True Conspiracy Theory

We are not fans of conspiracy theories. Most are ridiculous plots spun out of paranoid and sometimes malicious minds. Many end up harming people. If we accept the scriptural account, however, there's at least one conspiracy theory we must accept as fact. Like it or not, if we believe Scripture, we can't avoid the conclusion that this world has been seized by a cosmic force whose influence is everywhere and whose primary goal is to deceive. We don't mean to suggest that Satan is *directly* involved in everything. But if we accept the biblical view of the world, we have to grant that he's on some level involved in everything *insofar as it can be used as a means of getting people to believe lies rather than truth.*

The total package of lies that infiltrate our brains is "the pattern of this world"—what we are calling "the Matrix." Every message we've internalized, whether or not we're conscious of it, that tells us we are other than everything God says we are *is part of the Matrix.* Every mental image and every internal voice that arises in our minds that disagrees with the fact that we are full of God's love, joy, and peace *is part of the Matrix.* Every thought, impression, or feeling that is inconsistent with the truth that we are reconciled, forgiven, and made perfectly holy in Christ *is part of the Matrix.* Every feeling—rage, jealousy, fear, etc.—that motivates us to act in ways that are not consistent with God's design for our lives *is part of the Matrix.* Everything in our minds that disagrees with the fact that in Christ we are children of God, the radiant bride of Christ, and filled with all the fullness of God *is part of the Matrix.* And any assumptions about God or mental images of God we consciously or unconsciously hold that are other than that of a God of perfect love who died a hellish death just so he could spend eternity with us *is part of the Matrix.*

We need to realize that almost anything in this fallen world can be used to install Matrix lies in our brains. Morpheus spoke the truth when he told Neo, "The Matrix is everywhere. It is all around us."

The Matrix encompasses large elements of the media, for example. Most of the assumptions about God, the world, humans, and values implicit in today's movies and secular songs contradict truth as defined by Scripture. But the Matrix encompasses many other things as well. Family, friends, church, the Internet, things done to us, things done by us, random accidents, and just the meandering of our own fallen thought processes are all part of the Matrix of this world insofar as they are the means by which lies get installed in our minds.

Of course, the people who through word or deed speak lies into our lives are usually not intending to do so. In fact, they may be well-intentioned. It's just that, in a fallen world that is in bondage to Satan, even well-intentioned words and deeds can be used for destructive purposes.

This isn't paranoia. It's biblical truth!

Examples of the Matrix at Work

The father of a young girl I (Al) counseled routinely chided her about her appetite and her weight, especially during meals.[4] Though he perhaps was having a bit of misguided fun at her expense, he didn't mean any real harm. Indeed, he would say that he was trying to help her avoid growing up overweight. Ten years later this girl was still struggling, and the issue was one of survival because she was convinced that the most important thing in the world was to be thin. Though she had become dangerously underweight by avoiding food and exercising excessively, her self-image was distorted both in terms of what she actually looked like and what she felt she *should* look like. One of her internal pictures of herself was a terrifying, negative distortion of herself as an extremely overweight woman. At the same time, she held a positive distortion, an internal picture of her *ideal* self, possessing a body shape that would be impossible for her—and most women—to ever attain.

This poor woman was in a life-and-death struggle driven by the pattern of this world. She had internalized the Matrix media indoctrination aimed at little girls that convinces them if they want to be accepted, loved, and happy, they must look like a Barbie doll. It is a Matrix lie that torments many women and sometimes leads to death. This young woman was in bondage to a Matrix lie, and her father's words played a significant role in installing and perpetuating this lie.

When I (Greg) was not yet three years old, my grandmother brought home Christmas presents for my two sisters and brother, but none for me. Our mother had died six months earlier and so my grandmother was our primary caregiver. Unfortunately, I was hyperactive and she was very old, impatient, and cranky. So, not surprisingly, we didn't get along well. When my nine-year-old sister asked why no present was bought for me, my grandmother replied with a stern scowl on her face, "Greggie is a bad boy!"

My grandmother was simply frustrated with me and was undoubtedly trying her best to teach me a lesson. But I now look back on my life and can see how this message, which I received repeatedly, explains a good deal of my rebellious behavior growing up. My mental picture of myself and my internal communication about myself was that I was, in fact, "bad"—so bad I didn't deserve presents at Christmas. And my behavior reflected it.

I was to this extent imprisoned in the Matrix. My identity was to this extent defined not by God but by my grandmother. To this degree, I was enslaved to the god of this world, and the life God intended for me was being stolen and destroyed (John 10:10).

■ ■

God Wants You Free!

We can think of the Matrix as the total web of lies we've internalized that keep us living in contradiction to our true self—the self that is defined by God through Christ alone. And we need to know God wants us free from it. God wants us not just to *know about* abundant life; he wants us to *experience* abundant life. In contrast to the deceptive way we experience and understand God, the world, and ourselves within the Matrix, God wants us to experience for ourselves "what God's will is—his good, pleasing and perfect will" (Rom. 12:2). He wants us to experience, as part of our very self-identity, *his* love, *his* joy, *his* peace. He wants us to *really* live in Christ.

Jesus died to make this happen. He came to earth to destroy Satan and his works—his Matrix of lies—and to rescue humanity from his enslaving grasp (Heb. 2:14; 1 John 3:8). In terms of the movie *The Matrix, Jesus is the true Neo.* Through his death and resurrection, Christ defeated the powers of darkness and planted the mustard seed of the kingdom of God on this planet (Luke 13:18–19; Col. 2:11–15). God's kingdom expands every time a person surrenders his or her life to Christ and every time we take thoughts captive to Christ and replace lies with truth (2 Cor. 10:5). But insofar as we continue to believe, feel, and act on lies—despite the fact that we also believe the truth that Jesus is Lord—we remain in bondage. Hence the abundant life Jesus gave us is to this degree suppressed by lies.

If you're a follower of Jesus, you already have God's river of living water inside of you (John 7:38–39). It longs to gush forth as an explosion of Christlike love, freedom, and joy. But every lie that continues to exercise any influence in your mind corks it. So long as the deceptive voice of a father, grandmother, or anyone else continues to have a place in your mind, the river is to some extent blocked. To this extent, you are imprisoned in the Matrix.

Follow the White Rabbit

At the beginning of the movie *The Matrix*, Neo gets the message, "Follow the White Rabbit." He doesn't know what it means, but he is about to find out. A short while later Morpheus offers Neo the choice between a blue pill and a red pill. If Neo chooses the blue pill, he will go back to the illusory world of the Matrix. Morpheus tells him, "Take the blue pill and you wake up in your bed and believe whatever you want to believe." If he takes the red pill, however, "you stay in Wonderland, and I show you how deep the rabbit hole goes." Neo valiantly takes the red pill. He discovers the truth. He discovers freedom. For the first time in his life, he becomes something more than an extension of someone else's program.

We can go on believing whatever we want to believe. That's the comfortable route. It's also pure bondage. Or we can choose to follow the white rabbit, take the red pill, and see "how deep the rabbit hole goes." Following this path is sometimes difficult and, we will see, leads us into some strange territory. But it is the way to freedom. It leads us into "Wonderland." It leads us to the real world in which we experience as real and true all that God says is true.

At this point in this book we are merely on the precipice of the rabbit hole looking down. We haven't begun to fall yet. The power of the Matrix doesn't reside primarily in deceptive information. It resides in the way it sustains deception in our experience. It imprisons us not so much by information we consciously believe but by what we experience without even being conscious of it—indeed, often in direct contradiction to what we consciously believe. The Matrix contains information, but it is experienced as both real and true.

Yet, gaining information about how the Matrix runs and is structured is important. Indeed, before we can really plunge down the rabbit hole, we'll need to learn some things about our brains (chapter 2), the nature of thought (chapter 3), and the nature of the warfare in our minds (chapter 4). Only by understanding these things can we understand the Matrix, the power it has over us, and most importantly, the way to escape it.

"Would you like to know what [the Matrix] is?" Morpheus asks Neo. We are about to find out.

■ ■ ■ ■ ■ ■ ■ ■ ■ ■ ■ ■ ■ ■ ■ ■ ■ ■ ■ ▪ ▪ ▪ ▪ ▪

Exercise 1

Assessing Our Bondage to the Matrix

Following each chapter we will be suggesting one or more exercises for you to practice. These exercises are indispensable if you are to set your mind free to experience real life in Christ. "No one can tell you what the Matrix is," Morpheus tells Neo. *"You have to experience it for yourself."* He is exactly right!

Unless you learn to apply the principles taught in this book, it will be just another book giving you information. Information is important, but, as you probably already know, *information alone does not bring about transformation.* You need to *experience for yourself* the material taught in this book if it is to significantly help you escape the Matrix. We therefore strongly recommend that after you've completed each chapter, you stop and practice the exercise we provide to go along with that chapter.

In chapter 1 we defined the Matrix as the total package of lies that infiltrate our brains. The Matrix consists of every mental image and message we've internalized that disagrees with who we are in Christ. These images and messages all have an emotional component. So we may add that every emotion we experience that is inconsistent with our identity in Christ (e.g., rage, jealousy, fear, depression, hatred), as well as every behavior that is motivated by these emotions, is part of the Matrix.

We now want you to take some time to do a self-assessment. Conscious assessment is the first step in waking up to how you in particular are entrapped in the Matrix. We encourage you to honestly and prayerfully assess your life in terms of the four areas outlined below. Do this conscious assessment three separate times over the next week, and record what you find. This exercise will help you locate the primary areas in which you are entrapped in the Matrix and thus the primary areas you'll want to work on throughout this book.

1. *Ask God to help you honestly evaluate your life.* Do you regularly experience emotions that are inconsistent with your identity in Christ (e.g., stress, aggression, anger, anxiety, depression, hatred, fear)? Do you regularly engage in behaviors that are inconsistent with your identity in Christ (e.g., addiction to alcohol, tobacco, drugs, pornography, or gambling)? Do you have physical symptoms that reflect something may not be right with your life—issues like migraine headaches, ulcers, high blood pressure, fibromyalgia, chronic fatigue? (We are aware that many physical symptoms are the result of physiological conditions and not psychosomatic in nature. However, record anything you find.)

2. *Prayerfully and honestly investigate what Matrix beliefs you may now be embracing.* For example, do you ever think things like: "I am worthless"; "I am stupid"; "I am no good"; "I can never win"; "I will never change"; "God has favorites, and I am not one of them"; "If I try harder, God will love me more"; or, "I have committed the unpardonable sin"? Record anything you find.

3. *Prayerfully assess yourself as to any fears you may have that in any way interfere with God's goal of having you live a full, healthy, and passionate life.* Some of the most common are the fears of public speaking, of social settings, of engaging in conflict with others, or of disappointing others. A certain percentage of people may have phobias attached to things such as clowns, insects, flying, being in open spaces, etc. Record anything you find.

4. *Honestly ask yourself if you are unable to enter into or maintain committed or intimate relationships.* Also, do you have trouble respecting the boundaries of others or maintaining healthy boundaries for yourself? Record any observations you have about this.

After each time you evaluate these four areas, review your answers and see if you can discern a theme or pattern to them. For example, a person might discern a connection between a belief that he or she isn't lovable, a fear of social settings, and an inability to enter into intimate relationships. In light of this investigation, decide on the one or two things on which you are going to work most intently throughout this book. As you read this book, ask yourself: how does the material I'm reading apply to the Matrix belief, emotion, attitude, or behavior I've decided to work on at this point in my life? Write down the one or two Matrix aspects of your life you want to be freed from as a result of reading and working through this book.

2

Interpreting Electrical Signals

The Magnificent Brain and Its Neural-Nets

MORPHEUS: What is real? How do you define real? If you're talking about what you can feel, what you can smell, what you can taste and see, then "real" is simply electrical signals interpreted by your brain. This is the world that you know. . . . It exists now only as part of a neural-interactive simulation that we call the Matrix. You've been living in a dream world, Neo. . . .

What is the Matrix? Control. The Matrix is a computer-generated dream world built to keep us under control in order to change a human being into this [holds up a battery].

—————⊗⊗⊗—————

For as he thinks within himself, so he is.

Proverbs 23:7 NASB

People are slaves to whatever masters them.

2 Peter 2:19 NRSV

Deeper than Knowledge or Will

You don't consistently experience the abundant life the Bible says you should have. You are not "filled to the measure of all the fullness of God" (Eph. 3:19). Like a splinter in your mind, you know something is amiss, but you don't know what. You thought it was perhaps a lack of knowledge, so you read some books. You thought it might be a lack of willpower, so you strove to the point of exhaustion. These may have helped. Yet you still have the splinter.

You *know* a lot and *work* a lot but *experience* little. Why?

The most fundamental reason is because the Matrix is much deeper than our conscious beliefs or willpower. It goes down to our most basic assumptions about reality—assumptions we've probably held most of our lives; assumptions we've probably never questioned or even noticed. So far we've been applying informational Band-Aids to cure a brain tumor. It's time for some radical surgery.

"The Matrix is everywhere," Morpheus tells Neo. *This* is the problem. We are *in* the Matrix, and the Matrix is *in* us. Like the nose on our face, it's too close to notice. Its imprisoning power lies in its subtlety. Even when we catch glimpses of who we truly are in Christ, under the persistent impact of this systemic delusion, we immediately forget (James 1:24).

The question we have to answer is: *how do we escape?* In terms of the movie, what does "taking the red pill" look like?

Now in real life, as opposed to the Hollywood film (and some quick-fix pop therapies), getting free from the Matrix involves much more than just taking a pill. It *starts* there, for sure. You have to be sick of being defined by your past, sick of being a conformist to the "pattern of the world," and tired of the splinter in your brain. And yes, you must decide. This takes resolve. You definitely need to take the red pill.

But the actual process of escaping the Matrix is more like the process Neo had to go through in order to rescue humankind from their bondage to an illusory world. Neo had to first believe that the Matrix was real, that the Matrix exists. And then Neo had to learn how to fight in the Matrix. He had to learn the rules that governed the Matrix and learn how to bend them to his advantage. Neo had to learn to escape the lies that held him in bondage to replace the lies with truth. Our task is very much like his.

Our ultimate mission is to get free from the Matrix that presently controls our minds and therefore our lives. Our mission, given to us by God, is to "demolish strongholds"—everything that is in disagreement with our knowledge of God, his world, and his salvation—and "take captive every thought to make it obedient to Christ" (2 Cor. 10:4–5). It is not an easy task, but with God's help and a firm resolve, it *is* doable.

To begin our training, it will be helpful to learn a bit about how God designed our brains, learn the rules that govern them, and discover how the Matrix of the world has infiltrated them. For the rules that govern the Matrix are simply the rules that govern our brains.

Interpreting Electrical Signals

In the movie *The Matrix*, humanity is enslaved in a neural-interactive simulation world. It is a virtual-reality world created by an artificial intelligence controlling the neurons in people's brains. One of the reasons the movie is intriguingly plausible is that this premise is not impossible. It is, in fact, based upon how the brain is designed by God to function. For the truth is that *our entire sense of reality is formed by the neurological activity in our brains*.

Morpheus speaks an illuminating truth when he informs Neo that everything we sense as real is "simply electrical signals interpreted by your brain. This is the world that you know." In truth, we have no access to "reality" other than through (or better, "as") the electrical-chemical signals in our brains.

To illustrate, you believe you're reading a book right now. But what you're directly experiencing is an electrical-chemical reaction in your brain—neurons firing on other neurons in patterned ways (forming a "neural-net"). The room you're in right now, the chair you're sitting on, every sound you're hearing, every smell you're smelling, and every taste you're tasting—all are networks of neurons firing in your brain.

Of course, if you're remotely sane you believe that there's an *actual* book, an *actual* room, etc., triggering these neurons to fire in ways that accurately reflect the outside world. But the point is, you only know what's *outside* because of what's going on *inside*. Morpheus was right. Your experience of this moment *is* a mass of electrical-chemical signals in your brain.

We are, in a sense, trapped within our skulls. We are as dependent on our brains for our information about the outside world as a person surfing the Internet is dependent on his or her computer. We only know what it tells us, which is why it's conceivable that the ultimate cause of some of our neurological activity is something other than the real world. It's conceivable that an artificial intelligence—or rebellious principality and power (Rom. 8:38; 2 Cor. 2:11; Eph. 6:12)—is deceiving us. It's conceivable that some things we experience as "real" are rooted in falsehoods.

Not only is this conceivable but, as we saw in the last chapter, this is in fact what is happening, according to Scripture. To one extent or another, we are conformed to a Matrix of the world, are governed by the cosmic deceiver, and thus experience reality as other than it really is. But because the only reality we know is the one given in our activated neurons, we have no neurological way to distinguish what is merely experienced as real and what is *in fact* real—that is, what is in fact *true*.

This is what keeps us in bondage to lies. To the extent that our neurons fire according to falsehoods, we are, like the humans in the movie *The Matrix*, ignorantly held captive by illusions. We automatically assume our neurologically constituted experience reflects truth, when in fact it does not.

It will be helpful at this point to take a closer look at how our brains function, for this is the computer we rely on to surf the Internet of the real world. This will help us appreciate more fully how the circuitry of this computer works in our favor when it runs on the right programs and what we need to do to alter it when it's running on the wrong programs.[1]

The Complexity and Power of Our Organic Computer

In all God's creation there is nothing as awesome and mysterious as the human brain. It weighs only three and a half pounds, but this little organic computer can in most respects outperform the largest and most sophisticated computers humans have been able to construct.

Consider that one gram of this gray matter (roughly the size of a pea) is more complex than the entire global telephone system. The average adult brain consists of more than 10 billion neurons communicating with one another through more than 10 trillion synaptic connections. (Synaptic connections are the junctions or gaps between the axon and the dendrite of a neuron. The biochemical neurotransmitters are released from the axon to stimulate and communicate with the dendrite of a second neuron.) As unbelievable as it sounds, the number of possible neuronal connections in the brain is more than all of the stars in the known universe (approximately 50 billion galaxies with an average of 100 billion stars each). Although the average dendrite is a fraction of a millimeter in size, if you were to line up all the dendrites in your brain, the line would circle the globe five times!

The brain registers particular experiences or produces particular thoughts by firing in certain patterned ways with its billions of neurons connected by its trillions of synapses. The magnitude of this complexity is beyond comprehension. Among other things, we simply have trouble thinking in terms of *trillions*. Fortunately, the brain communicates much faster than you can possibly count, and it operates along millions of neurological pathways all at once. Were this not the case, it would take several lifetimes to think a single thought!

The feats the brain is capable of are even more amazing than its astounding complexity. At this very moment your brain is accessing its memory files to identify each mark on this page as a meaningful letter, each collection of letters as a meaningful word, each collection of words as a meaningful sentence, each collection of sentences as a meaningful paragraph, and so on. During this process, you're being impacted by an estimated 100 million bits of information per second. The reticular activating system of your brain deletes 98 percent of this while the rest of your brain filters the remaining 2 million bits of information. From all of this, your brain brings to your conscious awareness only the five to nine pieces of information per second it believes is most relevant to you at the moment.

For example, you probably weren't consciously aware of the weight of your buttocks pressing against the chair on which you're sitting until we just now made that piece of information relevant to you by having you read this sentence. That means that the original five to nine pieces of information that you were consciously attending to changed. You had to let go of one of the chunks of data in order to consciously attend to the weight of your derriere against the chair, which you are doing again right now. Though you only became conscious of your weight on the chair when we mentioned it, your brain was already monitoring it at an unconscious level.

We could have just as easily turned your attention to your rate of breathing, to the sounds outside your window, to various odors you may be smelling, to the beating of your heart, or to the color of whatever occupies the upper left corner of your peripheral vision at this moment. The brain is perpetually taking it all in, processing it, and offering your conscious self a mere fraction of this information. Every time you change your conscious focus, you alter the five to nine pieces of information to which you are consciously attending.

As we said earlier, every distinct aspect of your experience is a particular pattern of neurons firing on one another—what is referred to as a neural-net. A neural-net is activated in response to appropriate stimuli sometimes referred to as a "trigger." For example, you know what the word *trigger* means because your brain has been programmed to activate a distinct neural-net that identifies these markings (*t-r-i-g-g-e-r*) as having a particular meaning. *You're interpreting electrical signals.*

Actually, it's a bit more complex than that. What's actually happening is that light is being reflected off the markings on this page with a particular vibration. These vibrations are stimulating your eye in a particular fashion that is then sending a pattern of electromagnetic activity into your nervous system and up to your brain. This pattern of electromagnetic activity is triggering a distinct neural-net that is being interpreted as having a specific meaning. And all of this is happening automatically, according to a pre-established program (that is, your past learning) at a minute fraction of a second.

So it has been for every word you've read in this book thus far. And at every moment your brain was at the same time deleting

100 million pieces of data and processing 2 million other pieces of data. Without this designed ability to delete the vast amount of superfluous information we would not be able to function. You can see it's no exaggeration to say that there is nothing in the known universe that compares to the human brain. In fact, despite the remarkable advances neuroscience has made in the last two decades, much of the brain's magnificent complexity is yet a mystery. For example, we are not much closer to understanding how the brain produces consciousness than we were a century ago. How is this three-and-a-half-pound physical organism able to consciously reflect on and even alter what it is thinking about? How are we able to become aware of and modify what we see, hear, and sense in our heads? We do not know.

In fact, some neuroscientists—and many others—believe that our ability to consciously modify our thoughts requires that we accept that we are *more* than our physical brain. As Jeffery Schwartz has recently argued, it's not clear how we can explain the power of consciousness *over* neurological activity if consciousness is itself nothing more than neurological activity.[2] As the Bible attests, we are more than our brains; we are spirit. And the most amazing and least understood aspect of the brain is its ability to interact with the spirit.

All the remaining chapters, in one way or another, address the issue of how we as spirit-beings can program the brain's neurological circuitry in accordance with truth. But first we need to become aware of how the magnificent efficiency of this neurological circuitry works against us when we *don't* consciously take authority over it.

On Becoming a Robot

We've seen that our total sense of reality at any moment is the result of the brain's remarkable *synthesis* of activated neural-nets. This experienced synthesis operates a bit like the way the single moving picture on your television screen is created by thousands of individual, minute light bulbs flickering on and off. Our brains synthesize the millions of patterned neurological reactions occurring at any given moment to produce our unified sense of reality in the here-and-now.

From the outside looking in, activated neural-nets are seen as weblike electrical firings in the brain. But as *you* experience these millions of neurons firing at any given moment, *it is the whole of your reality.*

Now things begin to get really interesting when you realize that you did not install most of the information that is stored in the neural-nets that comprise your brain. Which means, you didn't choose to have most of your neurons fire the way they do. You have distinct neural-nets for doing math, loving people, hating people, processing verbs, experiencing fear, feeling jealousy, and having faith in God. Indeed, you have distinct neural-nets for every possible emotion you could experience as well as every activity in which you could engage. And most of these neural structures you did not purposefully or consciously install.

Nor did you consciously install most of the triggers that activate these neural-nets. For example, you didn't choose to have the markings *t-r-i-g-g-e-r* stimulate the neural-net that gives meaning to these markings. You *inherited* this neural-net that is linked to this trigger, as you did most of your neural-nets and triggers. Someone or something installed these for you. And since your whole sense of reality is rooted in these neural-nets, it follows that *your whole sense of reality at any given moment has been largely determined by other people and outside events.*

Once installed, these neural-nets operate automatically and deterministically—remember, they're just organic transmitters of electromagnetic energy—and they do so faster than your conscious mind can ordinarily grasp.[3] For example, you did not have to think about the meaning of the markings when they were triggered. The neural-net that gives meaning to these particular markings operates on autopilot, as it were. Once it is installed, these markings will continue to deterministically and automatically activate the organic transmitters of electromagnetic energy associated with them until the brain is reprogrammed to do otherwise.

This God-given, deterministic, autopilot aspect of the brain is actually a wonderful gift, for it allows us to process information quickly, efficiently, and accumulatively. We don't have to keep learning things over and over again. The brain neurologically stores conclusions it has reached and treats these *as reality* until it is instructed to do otherwise. You instantly know the meaning of every word you're reading right now only because of this. This mind-boggling efficiency and stability works to our advantage when our neurons have been programmed to fire in ways that communicate truth and that are beneficial to us.

But what if the coded information that has been installed in our neurons is not true and is not helpful? What if an installed neural-net contains meaning that is completely out of sync with what God tells us is true? Now the remarkable efficiency of our brains that God intended for our advantage *works against us.* Think about this for a minute or two. *The brain processes and installs falsehoods with the same efficiency and stability with which it processes truth.*

As automatically as you understand the words you're reading right now, you will experience as real something that is not real *if an activated neural-net tells you so.* And you will not notice it any more than you noticed your brain retrieving the meaning of the words you're reading right now. You will to this extent be in bondage to the efficiency of your brain and be trapped in a deceptive virtual reality. Not only this, but to this extent you will have been reduced to an automated, programmed, deterministic extension of whoever or whatever installed these neural-nets.

You are to this degree imprisoned in the Matrix. You are to this degree a slave, for "people are slaves to whatever masters them" (2 Peter 2:19 NRSV).

The Architect's Installation of a Matrix Neural-Net

As we shall see in more depth in part 2 of this work, one of the primary ways the Architect (Satan) keeps us in bondage to the Matrix is by using God's design to install memories that contain painful lies. Under the right triggers, traumatic experiences of the past are automatically, and in a fraction of a second, reexperienced in a vivid, holographic manner.[4] This reexperiencing the event includes the *emotional content* and *meaning* of the memory. Whatever meaning your brain gave to the experience when it first occurred (e.g., "men are dangerous"; "sex is dirty"; "I'm not important") is reexperienced *as true* in the present.

An experience from my (Al's) childhood illustrates how this works. My father was a terrible alcoholic who died in a bar fight when I was eight years old. Due to the physical, sexual, and emotional abuse I experienced as a boy, I have amnesia about the first nine years of my life. One of the few childhood memories I have took place about a year before my father's death. Quite uncharacteristically, he asked me to go on a walk with him. It was a beautiful summer day, and I remember feeling excited. I thought to myself, "This must be what normal dads do with their sons," and it felt good.

My excitement was short-lived, however. We came upon a boy who was a couple of years older than me and known to be a bully in our neighborhood. To my horror, my father called this boy over and asked him to fight with me! To my amazement, the ten-year-old said no. I heard a little voice inside me say, "Thank you, God, for helping me." Then, as if in slow motion, I heard my dad tell the boy that he'd give him a quarter if he'd fight me. To a ten-year-old in 1956, a quarter was a lot of money. The bully quickly sized me up, saw I was no match for him, and proceeded to beat me up. My father watched as this boy gave me a swollen black eye and a bloody nose. He finally intervened, shaking his head and muttering to himself, "Just what I thought."

I now suspect that, in his own twisted way, my father was trying to teach me about the need to be tough in a world where, in his view, toughness was a prerequisite to survival. My father hung with a very tough bar crowd, and the only thing that garnered respect in this toxic world was his ability to hold his liquor and beat up others. What my father was trying to discern, I believe, was whether I had what it took to survive in this violent world. I failed his toxic test, and a Matrix belief that I did not measure up was installed.

This event became one of the defining events in my life. I resolved I would never lose a fight again. I accepted my father's view of the world as a horrible, violent, perpetually threatening place. I became convinced that the strong do not protect the weak; they prey on them. Through the abuse at the hands of my father as well as others, I became convinced that those who "love" you are going to hurt you. The meaning of *love*, for me, was pain. I became convinced that to be perceived as weak was dangerous.

Under the right triggers, the memory of my eight-year-old beating would be instantly and repetitively replayed in my mind in a vivid, holographic fashion. I was living out the implications of being stuck in the Matrix. I would thus interact with the world largely as an angry, terrified eight-year-old. I became a prisoner within the Matrix.

A good portion of the next two decades of my life was spent avoiding the feeling of shame, hiding my fears, and expressing my rage. To this extent I was defined by my dysfunctional, alcoholic father and not by our Father in heaven. The magnificent efficiency of my brain was working as God designed, but it was working against me. As long as these thoughts and emotions could get externally triggered, I would remain a prisoner of the Matrix, enslaved by the god of this world.

The Good News is that what the enemy intends for evil, God can use for good (Gen. 50:20). The Bible tells us that in all things—however evil and damaging they may be—God is at work to bring about good (Rom. 8:28). God doesn't *cause* terrible things to happen to us. Such things ultimately are part of the Architect's schemes, not God's. But if we will cooperate with him, God wisely and creatively works all things to our advantage and to the benefit of the kingdom of God.

Life in the Matrix is a perpetual cycle of triggers and deterministically activated neural-nets that we did not choose to have installed. But God created a way for us to break this cycle. Not only can we survive our past experiences and bondages, we can flourish. As Paul puts it, we can become "more than conquerors" (Rom. 8:37). In his infinite wisdom, God can actually turn our tragedies, even our past failures, to our favor so that we become more than we otherwise would have been. In the hands of our wise and loving Father, past tragedies and failures become learning experiences and even our qualifications for particular ministries.

As I look back on my life, I can discern the loving hand of God gradually leading me out of my Matrix beliefs. Through my wife, my children, and many others, I learned how to love, to trust, and to accept my apparent weaknesses. Through my own struggles I learned how to collapse Matrix lies and install truth. I have learned that the cognitive structures of our Matrix neural-nets *can* be changed and aligned with the truth of God's Word and his Spirit. Indeed, I have learned that the most powerful force upon this planet occurs when an individual is in alignment with God's Spirit.

Again, it was not God's will that I was beaten and humiliated as a little boy. His heart grieved for me, as it does over tragic events that some of you have experienced. But you need to know that God is never at a loss as to how he can use evil intentions and painful events to accomplish something good and beautiful. No matter what the Architect of the Matrix does to define us, rob us of our dignity, or destroy our hopes and dreams, we can be more than conquerors when we align with truth.

"What is the Matrix?" Morpheus answered his own question: "Control." We are in bondage to the Matrix to the extent that our neurological activity—our thoughts, emotions, and therefore our behavior—are controlled by forces outside ourselves. We are freed from the Matrix when we submit our minds to God's loving authority, work with him to bring good out of evil, and regain the control over our brains that he always intended us to have.

Debugging the Brain of Neurochips

It might be useful to think of a neural-net as something like a microchip that was implanted in your brain by someone or some event in your life. (For the sake of clarity, we'll henceforth refer to these lie-encoded neural-nets as *neurochips*.) Under the right circumstances—the right trigger—the neurochip is activated. Once activated, it deterministically communicates a message and creates a feeling as part of its message, and it does so in a fraction of a second, beneath the level of consciousness. To the extent dictated by the neurochip, you are a slave, a neurochip-controlled robot that will experience reality according to whomever or whatever installed the neurochip in you.

A neurochip that re-presents you as a loser getting beaten up is activated whenever you're in circumstances you perceive as threatening. A neurochip that screams, "You're fat!" gets activated at the sight of food. A neurochip that re-presents a grandmother growling, "You're bad," gets activated whenever you want attention. To this extent you're reduced to a function of the programming of whomever or whatever installed the life-sucking neurochip in your brain.

The first question Morpheus asks Neo is, "Do you believe in fate?"

"No," Neo responds. "I don't like the idea that I'm not in control of my life." Yet, as Neo is about to learn, most of his life up to that point had been predetermined. His existence had been largely controlled from birth. For *whoever or whatever controls the neurons controls the life.* Our situation isn't all that different from Neo's. We have neurochips in our brains creating in us a sense of reality that contradicts reality as God defines it—that contradicts truth. Until we wake up to this fact and do something about it, we are largely reduced to the level of the prisoners of *The Matrix.*

A Phobic Neurochip

Just so we fully understand what we're dealing with, let's look at another real-life example of a neurochip in action.

In most respects Doreen was the kind of woman most people admire. She was intelligent, godly, successful, and attractive. But there was one thing about Doreen that significantly complicated and undermined the quality of her life as well as the lives of all who loved her. Doreen had an outlandish fear of insects. We're not talking about your run-of-the-mill "I hate spiders" sentiment. No, Doreen experienced absolute *terror* at the sight of bugs! In fact, she could be thrown into hysterics at the very possibility of confronting an insect.

Christians sometimes think the *pattern of the world* is just about morally significant things—our problems with lust, hatred, greed, and the like. But the Matrix is about anything and everything that to any degree keeps the quality of our lives beneath the *abundant life* God created us to have and Jesus died for us to have.

A Holy-Spirit-filled, more-than-a-conqueror child of the King of Kings ought not to be terrorized by insects! Doreen's phobia was a means of stealing, killing, and destroying part of her life (John 10:10). Doreen could not walk on grass, for that is where bugs live. She had trouble going out on warm, sunny days. She would not travel to "buggy" regions of the world, either on vacation or for work. She was obsessive about checking the house for bugs. She thought about bugs almost every day, and on certain days almost all day long! Aside from short respites during the coldest months of the year, this woman lived in perpetual anxiety.

How did this happen? A neurochip had been installed in Doreen by her mischievous little brother. As a nine-year-old, Doreen had fallen asleep face down on a lawn chair in her backyard. Meanwhile, her brother had been on an expedition collecting grasshoppers in a jar. Then he happened upon his sleeping sister.

Doreen woke up to find grasshoppers stuffed in the back of her blouse. Not being able to see them, she imagined herself covered with spiders, beetles, centipedes, and every other gross bug she'd ever seen. As her brother laughed hysterically, Doreen went into an absolute panic. Her nine-year-old brain instantly amplified the threat of the insects, and she was convinced she was being devoured by flesh-eating bugs. It also concluded that all insects were extremely dangerous and must be avoided at all costs.

A neurochip had been installed. From this point on, the autopilot of Doreen's brain would vigilantly maintain this Matrix belief and send a strong warning message whenever it sensed the possibility of coming into contact with an insect. For Doreen, the neurologically generated meaning of insects—and anything associated with her traumatic experience of insects—would be *death*. Given the right triggers, the meaning would automatically and deterministically be activated.

Thirty years later Doreen's magnificent brain, via this neurochip, was still trying to do its job: namely, protect Doreen from terrorizing, flesh-devouring insects. The trouble, of course, is that this neural-net was rooted in a lie. It was functioning as a Matrix neurochip. It was still operating from the uninformed and immature perspective of a terrorized nine-year-old rather than an intelligent, mature thirty-nine-year-old. When the right triggers were present, the neurochip was activated, and Doreen reexperienced the terror of a nine-year-old covered with all kinds of bugs.

Once triggered, Doreen "knew" insects were going to eat her as automatically as you know the meaning of the words you're reading right now. At the sight of a bug, Doreen "knew" as certainly and as intensely as when it originally happened that she would die. She "knew" this without consciously thinking about it—*which is why conscious information about bugs would not do any good to help her out of her phobia.* For as with all of us, Doreen's conscious mental process is hundreds of times slower than her unconscious mental process.[5]

This is the primary reason consciously held information does not translate into transformation. The neurochips are simply too fast.

■ ■
Waking Up to Our Imprisonment

As we've said, the remarkable efficiency of the brain works to our advantage when our neurological programming is in accord with truth. This is what God designed it for. But as we've now learned, this efficiency works against us when our programming is not in accordance with truth. To the extent that deceptive neurochips have been installed in us, we experience reality as other than it truly is. We are to this extent prisoners of our own mind, chained in ways we did not choose. Our prison was largely chosen for us. We are slaves, for as Peter said, "People are slaves to whatever masters them" (2 Peter 2:19 NRSV).

Now here's the real kicker. Our brains are *filled* with these neurochips. The same thing that caused Doreen's brain to suppress the truth about insects and instead experience terror causes us to automatically suppress multitudes of other truths and experience reality as other than it truly is.

If you don't experience yourself as a Spirit-filled child of the King who has an abundant River of Living Water, Joy, and Peace flowing out of you, this is evidence of Matrix neurochips in your organic computer. If you can't get free from desiring pornography, this is evidence of your neurological bondage. If you have a chronic need for attention, for approval, or for being right, this is further evidence that you're still under the thumb of persons and events in your past. Do you have trouble trusting others? Are you afraid of taking risks? Do you have an uncanny ability to sabotage relationships just as they're taking off? Do you have a need to control people? Are you sometimes overwhelmed with anger? All of this is evidence that you are yet living as an obedient puppet to the masters who installed neurochips in your brain. You're obediently carrying out someone else's program.

It's all about the way we experience reality when triggered by certain situations. It's all about neurochips. It's all about how we are conformed to the Matrix of this world (Rom. 12:2).

As we saw in chapter 1, Scripture tells us that in Christ we are loved, holy, redeemed, and filled with God's Spirit. It tells us we are given God's joy, peace, fearlessness, and many other wonderful things. But we don't experience this consistently. If we believe that God is telling us the truth in Scripture, then we *have* to conclude that it is our *experience*, not *God*, that is deceiving us. And, as we have seen, our experience is rooted in the electrical-chemical firings in our brains. Thus, every single aspect of the life of a person who trusts in Christ that doesn't conform to God's truth *must be assessed as due to neurochips*. We have been conformed to the Matrix of this world (Rom. 12:2). We have been deceived (2 Cor. 11:3). We have been blinded (2 Cor. 4:4). We are being controlled (1 John 5:19). Though we are in principle set free in Christ, we experience ourselves as slaves (2 Peter 2:19).

This ought to make you mad! Your anger should not be so much directed at those who installed the neurochips in your mind—most of them probably meant well and were just operating out of their own neurochips. Your anger should be directed at the prison in which you find yourself and at the master Architect, who uses God's miraculous design to orchestrate his evil intentions (1 Cor. 9:27; 15:9; Eph. 6:12). Hold onto that anger. If used right, it can fuel the intensity of your resolve to get free of this prison. And, as you will later learn, you're going to need all the intensity you can get.

The prison is the Matrix—the total constellation of our neural-net installations insofar as these neural-nets do not communicate truth. It's the polluted and deceptive aspect of our brains' synthesis of millions of neurological firings each moment. It is the total pattern of untruths we have at various times in our lives internalized as truth. It is our sense of reality insofar as this reality does not align with God's truth. And it forms our experience of our self-identity insofar as our identity is defined by the world and lies rather than by God and truth.

Morpheus was right. The Matrix really is everywhere. Indeed, the Matrix is within us. It's within our mothers, within our fathers, our friends, the media, the culture, past and present experiences, our own reasoning processes—it's every message we've ever internalized from any source *insofar as these messages are not true.*

We experience these messages as real, but they are not true. And this is our bondage.

Going Farther down the Rabbit Hole

We're still dealing mostly at the level of conceptual information. We've talked about what the Matrix is, how it operates, and how it keeps us in bondage by staying beneath the radar screen of our conscious awareness. But there's one more absolutely central aspect of the Matrix we need to understand. It is the aspect that most theories and approaches to transformation fail to understand. It is the aspect that most closely corresponds to the *Matrix* movies.

The Matrix is an experienced virtual reality—for this is how we are designed to think. We shall explore the holographic, experiential nature of our internal world in the next chapter. The rabbit hole goes deep indeed.

Exercise 2

Becoming a Detective of Your Mind

All transformation involves the alteration of neural-nets. Until we change the automatically triggered images, words, and sensations that constitute our internal virtual reality, we will not change. You can gather all the information you want, wish all you want, punish yourself all you want, and even pray all you want. But until your inner world is transformed, you are not transformed.

This is why Paul tells us that the main task of spiritual warfare is not trying to change our behavior through willpower; it's to take every thought captive to Christ (2 Cor. 10:5). To be transformed, we must renew *our minds* (Rom. 12:2; Eph. 4:22–23). The command for us to take our thoughts captive presupposes that we are more than our thoughts and that it is *our job* to take thoughts captive. We are commissioned and empowered to detect and eliminate Matrix neurochips in our brains.

To accomplish this, we must learn to *become detectives of our minds*. We have to develop the capacity to examine the images, words, and feelings of our inner world with the same objectivity and investigative curiosity as a detective. We must learn how to step outside of (disassociate from) our thoughts and observe them. For so long as we are associated to (identified with) our thoughts, we cannot hope to control them. They are controlling us.

The goal of this chapter's exercise is to help us begin to detect neurochips. It is designed to empower us to become detectives of our own minds. We want to begin to become experts at detecting thoughts and feelings that are not in alignment with what God says is true about us.

One helpful strategy to empower us to step outside of our internal world in order to observe it like a detective is to address it in the third person. The New Testament sometimes refers to the thoughts and emotions that constitute our internal world as our *soul* (psyche). By talking to your soul in the third person (e.g., by saying, "Soul, listen up . . . ," see Luke 12:17–21), we gain a disassociated (detached, objective) perspective. We isolate and empower that part of us that is more than our thoughts and emotions.

To this end, carefully read the following brief sampling of things Scripture says are true about you because of your faith in Christ. Speak each verse to your soul. Say, "Soul, listen up. Because of what Jesus did for me, I am . . . ," and then recite the truth of the verse. After each verse you've spoken to your soul, close your eyes and vigilantly and patiently wait for your soul to respond. Attend carefully to what you hear, see, or feel inside yourself when you speak the truth of the verse to yourself. You may have to do this several times before you detect your soul's response.

To illustrate, the Bible says that because of what Jesus did for you, you are filled with the peace and joy of God (John 14:27; Rom. 14:17). So in your mind, say, "Soul, listen up. Because of what Jesus did for me, I am filled with the peace and joy of the Lord." Then listen to what your soul does in response. You might hear a voice say something like, "No, you don't have peace and will never have peace." You might see an image of yourself being anxious and/or depressed. Or you might experience a feeling of shame or despair. If you hear, see, or feel anything that is not in complete agreement with the biblical truth you spoke to your soul, you can know that you have just detected a neurochip.

Conversely, when you speak this truth to your soul, you may hear words, see images, and experience feelings that *confirm* the truth you spoke. You might hear a voice say, "Yes, the peace of God passes all understanding." You might see yourself full of joy and peace. Or you might sense a peace and joy within. Such responses are one indication that, concerning this specific truth, your soul is "captive" to Christ (2 Cor. 10:5).

Now, don't get overconfident when your soul has within it neural chips that confirm biblical truths. Scripture commands us to be *vigilant* in detecting our innermost thoughts and feelings (our "heart," Prov. 4:23). You might find that when you speak this truth to your soul at a different time, some opposition arises. We need to understand that the Matrix is as complex as the brain it seeks to control. Hence, there are many variables that affect the response we get when we speak truth to our souls at any given moment.

One further preliminary word needs to be said. When you detect neurochips, resolve not to allow any part of yourself to get angry or frustrated at what you hear, see, and/or feel. Negative responses usually only bind us more strongly to the Matrix lies to which we are responding. At this point in our journey, simply *notice and record* the internal response and know that it is not true, however real and accurate it may presently feel. Recite the biblical truth to your soul once again and move on. We shall in subsequent chapters discuss strategies for collapsing these lies and installing truth.

"Soul, listen up. Because of Jesus Christ . . ."

Biblical truth	Identify what you saw, heard, and felt in response to the biblical truths		
	Saw	Heard	Felt
I am God's beloved child (John 1:12; Eph. 1:5).			

Biblical truth	Identify what you saw, heard, and felt in response to the biblical truths		
	Saw	**Heard**	**Felt**
I am completely forgiven, perfectly righteous, and free from condemnation (Rom. 5:1; 1 Cor. 6:20; Eph. 1:7).			
I am God's glorious temple and am filled with his fullness (1 Cor. 6:19; Eph. 3:19).			
I am holy and blameless (Eph. 1:4).			
I am the recipient of an eternal, infinitely rich inheritance (Eph. 1:11; 1 Peter 1:4).			
I am inseparable from God's love and will never be abandoned (Matt. 28:20; Rom. 8:35–39).	*Child*		*alone.*
I am the beautiful bride of Christ who ravishes the heart of God (Song of Songs 4:1–15; 6:4–9; Eph. 5:25–32).			
I am one over whom the Lord rejoices with singing (Zeph. 3:17).			
I am one for whom the Lord throws a party (Luke 15:7–10).			
I am indwelled by a fearless Spirit of love and self-control (2 Tim. 1:7).			
I am more than a conqueror in all things (Rom. 8:37).			

3

Entering the Matrix

Exploring the Nature of Thought

MORPHEUS: You are a slave, Neo. Like everyone else you were born into bondage. . . . A prison for your mind. . . . Unfortunately, no one can be told what the Matrix is. You have to see it for yourself.

—⊗⊗—

I am afraid that as the serpent deceived Eve by its cunning, your thoughts will be led astray from a sincere and pure devotion to Christ.

2 Corinthians 11:3 NRSV

Then you will know the truth, and the truth will set you free.

John 8:32

How is it that an intelligent woman can have all the correct information about insects yet live in terror of them? This question is no different than the question of how you and I experience ourselves in ways that contradict our knowledge about what the Bible says we are. The answer lies in the fact that the Matrix isn't constructed on theoretical information.

In the movie *The Matrix*, humanity wasn't held captive in a library of misleading books. They were held captive in a neurologically manipulated *illusory reality*. For Neo and Trinity to rescue humanity, they had to enter and wage war within this virtual reality. They had to fight by "bending the rules" of this reality.

It's time for us to explore what rules we need to bend. This chapter will begin to train you to become an effective detective of your mind. It is designed to raise your awareness of how you structure your thoughts to elicit various emotions, and it is intended to help you begin to discover the Matrix for yourself.

Morpheus was absolutely right. "No one can be told what the Matrix is. You have to *see it for yourself.*"

What's in a Memory?

Stop now and answer this simple question: what is in the backseat of your car? Please take the time to do this exercise. The more time you take to understand these new concepts the easier it will be to do the life-changing exercises later in the book! So consciously observe; be a detective of your mind. What is in the backseat of your car?

Got it? Now ask yourself: how did I do that? Thought processes are behaviors you *do*. They don't just happen. We want to help you discover how you *do* the thought process of remembering what is in the backseat of your car. How do you retrieve this information? You might be inclined to answer, "I did a search and activated neural-nets that store the sought-after information." While technically correct, that is *not* what we're asking. We're asking, *how* did you *do* the thought process of remembering what is in the backseat of your car? We're asking you to investigate the outcome of what you *experienced* when you did this cognitive search. How do you know what is in the backseat of your car so that you are able to answer the question "What is in the backseat of your car?"

You didn't see a ticker-tape strip of conceptual information flowing across the screen of your mind giving you the sought-after information, did you? As we've said, the brain doesn't think primarily with conceptual information. Rather, if you pay close attention, you'll notice that you *reexperienced* the backseat of your car. *This is how the brain thinks*. It replicates or re-presents (literally, makes present again) experienced reality.[1]

If you did "what's in the backseat of my car?" as Al did, you instantly saw a visual picture of your backseat. You saw it from the perspective of the front seat of the car. If you did it as Greg did, you saw the backseat looking in through the passenger side rear window. For Al the picture flashed for a fraction of a second. For Greg it lasted a while during which he lifted up a coat to see what was under it. For both of us the experience was in color, but Al's re-presentation was a snapshot while Greg's was a video.

Others may have investigated their backseat from the perspective of sitting in the backseat, and it may have been in black and white. For others the visual may have been so fast that you couldn't clearly make out anything on your internal screen. Yet you "just know" what's in the backseat. For still others, some sense other than visual may have stood out when you did, "what's in the backseat of my car?" For example, if you thought you smelled a rotting ham sandwich the last time you were in your car, you may have instantly experienced an internal odor in response to our question. If the last time you looked for something in your backseat was in the darkness of an unlit garage, you may have internally experienced what you *felt* at the time in response to our question.

Whatever happened inside of your brain in response to our question, this is *how you did* the memory of your backseat. We all do it differently. But we all have this in common: *we remembered by reexperiencing*. We re-present reality when we think.

Let's try another one. Recite the Lord's Prayer in your mind. (If you don't know it, try the Pledge of Allegiance.)

Okay, now say it to yourself again, but as you do, notice that you can hear each word of the Lord's Prayer (unless, of course, you are deaf, in which case you saw each word signed). If you did it as Al did, you heard each distinct word in your own voice.

Indeed, you could locate the voice as coming from a space between your mouth and your nose. If you did it as Greg did, you heard each word in your own voice but could not identify it coming from a specific location. Others may have heard the words of the Lord's Prayer in someone else's voice—your pastor, mother, or spouse. Some may have heard the voice from a specific location, like Al, while others did not, like Greg. For some it was soft; for others it was loud. Still others may have *seen* things in their minds as they heard the prayer. Greg saw an ancient script of the prayer; Al saw a re-presentation of God the Father as he said the prayer. Others may have seen a church, a stained-glass window, a Bible, or something else they associate with this prayer.

Again, what you experienced in your mind when remembering the Lord's Prayer was *how you did* this memory. We all did it somewhat differently. But we all did it *experientially*.

The two main points to get from these simple exercises is (1) that thought has a concrete, sensory, experiential structure made up primarily of internal sights, sounds, and feelings, and (2) we all do the structure of a memory uniquely.

Doing an Emotion

Let's follow the white rabbit down the hole a little deeper. This exercise will be a bit more involved. The previous two exercises helped you discover how you do a memory. This one will help you understand how you do an emotion.

We want you to *do* a pleasant memory. Take a moment and mentally re-present an event from your past that you consider fun, happy, or pleasant. It could be a vacation you went on, a time alone with a sweetheart, a past achievement, etc. As soon as you finish reading this sentence, we'd like you to stop reading and take time to get this pleasant memory vividly reexperienced in mind.

Got it? Okay. Hold the memory in mind and study it carefully. Notice how you are doing this behavior called "remembering a pleasant event." You're re-presenting the event to yourself, *as though it was presently real*, aren't you? You're internally replaying the pleasant memory in ways similar to how you initially recorded them. And notice that you're employing one or more of your five internal senses in your re-presentation of your past. Some are seeing pictures (visual) and/or hearing sounds (auditory). Some feel their bodies in the re-presentation (kinesthetic) and/or are smelling odors (olfactory). And a few may even be re-presenting something they tasted (gustatory). We shall refer to the way we employ our internal senses in re-presenting thought as "the VAKOG code" (Visual, Auditory, Kinesthetic, Olfactory, Gustatory).

No two people do a pleasant memory exactly alike. In fact, if two people experienced exactly the same pleasant event, their re-presentation of the memory would not be done in exactly the same way. The pleasant feelings you have about this particular memory are there because of the unique way you do this particular memory. What you saw, heard, felt, smelled, and/or tasted (the VAKOG external) is transformed into particular electromagnetic waves or a code you employ (VAKOG internal) in remembering the pleasantness of the event. Alter any of the specific distinctions of how you do this memory—that is, change the way you internally see, hear, feel, smell, or taste when you do this memory—and the feelings that surround this memory will change.

To discover some of these distinctions, keep the memory in mind as you answer the following questions.

1. *Do you see anything in this pleasant memory?*

Do you see anything on the screen of your mind when you do this pleasant memory? Most (but not all) of those reading this exercise will answer yes. Some will see their mental re-presentation very clearly at first, but then it will fade. Others can hold the visual in front of them easily and for as long as they decide to do so. But others don't see anything when they engage in the mental behavior called "doing a pleasant memory." Don't feel bad about this. It just means that you are among a certain percentage of people who didn't record their pleasant memories through visual re-presentation or that the visual part of the memory was so fast you couldn't notice it consciously. It just means that the *V* of your VAKOG code is not very relevant to the pleasantness of your memory.

2. *Is your pleasant memory in color, or is it in black and white?*

Keep the memory in mind. If you are seeing your re-presentation, is it in color, or is it in black and white? If it is in color, is the color vivid, or rather dull? Some may even find that their memory alternates between color and black and white.

3. *Is your pleasant memory moving, or is it a still frame?*

If you are seeing your re-presentation, is it like a photograph (still or snapshot), or is it moving, like a video? Examine it carefully. As with the previous question, some may find that their memory alternates between these two, moving for a bit and then stopping, only to start moving again. Others may find that they shuffle slides or see different movie clips of the pleasant memory. Still others may have yet a different visual component to the way they do their pleasant memory.

4. *Are you "associated" or "disassociated" to your pleasant memory?*

Do you experience your memory *through your own eyes*—that is, from the perspective you had when it originally occurred, as if you are there again? (This is called being "associated.") Or do you see yourself in the memory from a third-person perspective, as though you were seeing yourself in a video or seeing yourself on a photograph? (This is called being "disassociated.") You could also be part of the percentage of people who alternate between associated and disassociated re-presentations.

In seminars, we ask participants to indicate how many do their pleasant memories in an associated way and how many do them in a disassociated way. Typically, the group is divided about in half. We then ask, "If you saw yourself in the memory (disassociated), how do we know that the memory is less like it actually happened than if you experience the memory through your own eyes (associated)?" The question usually baffles people for a moment. After some reflection, however, they come to understand that their original experience couldn't have included seeing themselves from a third-person perspective. When we remember from a disassociated perspective, we are assuming a perspective we couldn't possibly have had at the time the memory occurred.

The point we're making is that all memories are cognitive maps to a territory.[2] Our re-presentations of what happened are never identical to what happened. They are rather cognitive constructs that enable us to experience what our brains think we need to experience—in this case, what is necessary for "doing a pleasant memory."

We might say that the territory of which our re-presentations are a map is not simply *what* happened but also *the meaning* of what happened. In forming a re-presentation of a pleasant memory, our brains know what aspects of our past experience to reproduce and highlight and which aspects can be ignored to allow us to experience a pleasant aspect of our past. (The VAKOG external of an event is transformed into our VAKOG internal.) The specific structures of the re-presentations (our internal VAKOG code) help us to reference one feeling from another.

If we had asked you to remember an *un*pleasant memory, the map would have been very different. The VAKOG code for this unpleasant memory would be different from the code of a pleasant one, for the meaning in this territory is different from the meaning in the territory of a pleasant memory.

As we shall see more clearly later on, our brains know how to do a memory—or any thought—in a specific way that elicits the meaning and attached emotion for which it is searching. If it is triggered to do "pleasant," it knows what to re-present and how to re-present it to be congruent with that emotion. If it is externally triggered to do "fear" or "shame," our brains know how to do that as well. In fact, every single emotion you presently do has a unique VAKOG code; this is the brain's way of referencing one emotion opposed to another emotion. If you change any of the internal VAKOG codes distinctions, you will change the emotion to some degree.

Why is all of this important? Because while we don't have the power to directly change our emotions, we *do* have the ability to change the re-presentations with which emotions are associated. We can't change fear, shame, jealousy, or any other emotion simply by willing it away. But we *are* able to permanently alter the re-presentations to which these emotions are associated. When we become detectives of our own minds and learn the specific ways our brains structure a particular emotion (the VAKOG code it employs in the re-presentation that includes the emotion), we will be able to choose to do it *or not.*

   5. *Do you hear anything in your pleasant memory?*

Re-present your pleasant memory again. Attend to it. Now notice whether or not there is any sound to your memory. If there is, is it loud or soft? In our experience only about ten to fifteen percent of people include sound in a pleasant memory. In these cases it is likely that sound was a significant part of the pleasantness of their past experience, hence their brain reproduces sound when the memory is triggered. It is the *A* (auditory) part of the VAKOG code of that re-presentation. Anyone who is not hearing impaired could remember the sound that was present at the time of an event they recall if they so desire. But the fact that sound wasn't present when they initially accessed their pleasant memory simply reveals that sound wasn't a part of their internal strategy for recalling this particular memory as being pleasant.

6. *How intense is the pleasantness of this memory?*

You feel a pleasant emotion when you re-present this memory, otherwise your brain wouldn't have accessed this memory in response to our initial question. Remember the pleasant memory once again and notice the feelings associated with it. Rate how intense the feeling of pleasantness is on a one-to-ten scale, one representing no feelings and ten representing extremely intense feelings of pleasantness. (This is called a *calibrated evaluative self-reference* and will later become an important detective tool for building awareness of how we escape the Matrix.)

Note that when we asked you to rate the intensity of this memory your brain had to unconsciously retrieve and automatically catalog other pleasant memories in order to calibrate the one we are assessing. Think about it. You could not have rated the pleasantness of your memory without first creating a reference system. If you rated the intensity of feeling at a seven, for example, your brain had to know that there are other pleasant memories with the intensity of six or eight.

7. *Do you experience anything else in your memory?*

Is there any other sense employed in your memory? For example, in one of Greg's fondest memories, he feels a cool breeze (kinesthetic) and can smell the ocean (olfactory) as he watches a bright orange sunset. In one of Al's memories—a handball match—he can feel the combination of all the senses (this is called "synesthesia"). Do you reexperience the feel of touch or smell or even reexperience the taste or anything else at the same time in your pleasant memory?

Each sense that is re-presented in thought—what you internally see, hear, feel, and so on—is called a *modality*. And every distinction that we might make about how we do sight, hearing, feeling, and so on in our thought is called a *submodality*. For example, if you see your pleasant memory, you are employing a visual modality (the V of VAKOG). Whether it is a snapshot or includes motion, black or white, color or muted, big or small, are a few of the submodality distinctions of visual modality. Our questions about whether there was color or movement, the intensity of feeling, and so on were meant to help you become conscious of your modality and submodality distinctions.

Recognizing how we do particular thoughts and particular emotions associated with these thoughts is very important. Until we become aware of how we actually do our emotionally laden thoughts, it will be difficult to gain control over them. When we learn and evaluate the modality and submodality distinctions that elicit particular emotions, it becomes possible to alter them.

We are more than our neurons and have the power to take thoughts, and therefore emotions, captive to Christ (2 Cor. 10:5; Rom. 12:2). But it's very difficult to capture and renew something of which we're not aware. We can wish and pray and promise all we want. But so long as we keep seeing, hearing, and sensing in our mind the virtual reality that is associated with our emotion, the emotion will not change. Indeed, it *cannot* change, for the emotion is part of the same neural-net we are seeing, hearing, and sensing.

More specifically, the emotion is the *meaning* dimension of what we are seeing, hearing, and sensing. The VAKOG code you elicit to do a particular thought is what it is precisely because this code contains a particular emotion. And this is why we said that you would change the "pleasantness" of your pleasant memory if you altered any of the modality and submodality distinctions you employ in having this particular pleasant memory.

The Five Senses Turned Inward

What all of this demonstrates is that we don't think primarily with conceptual information. We think with concrete, sensory information. We think by replicating reality on the inside. We quite literally *re-present*—make present again—our experience of the world when we have a memory. More technically, we reactivate the same network of neurons that were initially activated in our original experience, to some extent experiencing the event all over again. The reexperience or re-presentation will replicate the intensity of the original experience to the degree that our inner re-presentation is like the original experience—concrete, vivid, and with all our senses.

This isn't just true of memories. *It's how we generate our thoughts*. We think by concretely replicating sense experience on the inside. As authors Lakoff and Johnson put it, all thought is "embodied."[3] Even our most abstract and general thoughts are metaphorically rooted in our concrete, physical experience. Whenever we think, we in some way replicate aspects of our bodily experience of the world. We think by turning our sense experience of the world inward.

We didn't need modern cognitive philosophers or neuroscientists to tell us this. Almost everybody throughout history who has paid much attention to how we think has seen this. As far back as the fourth century BC, Plato described thought as an inner artist painting pictures on the soul.[4] His student Aristotle spoke of the mind as a sort of soft wax upon which impressions are made with our senses. (Today we know the "wax" consists of neurons.) When we think, Aristotle argued, we are viewing these impressions. He concluded that "the soul never thinks without a mental image."[5] With the exception of several decades of misguided thinking in the twentieth century, this has been an almost universally shared insight.

But don't accept this on the authority of Plato, Aristotle, or anyone else. It will remain mere information if you do. As Morpheus told Neo, you need to experience it for yourself.

Let's go deeper down the rabbit hole with a few more odd but important questions. Take a moment on each of these. They will help you become further acquainted with the nature of your inner virtual reality.

- What exactly do you expect to be doing tomorrow at noon? Become a detective of your mind. Investigate how you accessed this information.

- Think of one major thing you hope to accomplish before you die. What behavior did you *do* in your mind to answer this question?
- Think about someone you are mad at, mistrustful of, or worried about. What internal virtual reality world do you re-present that embodies this emotion?

Some of you may yet be insisting that you "just know" these things. We encourage you to dig deeper. Look within yourself more closely. No one "just knows" things. You *do* something to know things. We want you to discover *how* you do it. What do you mentally see, hear, and/or sense in response to the above questions? You have an internal VAKOG code to help you know how you do each one of these thoughts. Like everyone else, you think by turning your sense experience of the world inward.

The Deep Structure of Our Inner World

Let's follow the white rabbit still farther down the hole. This exercise is simple, but it makes an important point. What is the meaning of each of the following randomly selected words?

- elephant
- sun
- father
- music
- church
- vomit

Now remember, thinking is a behavior we do. Giving meaning to markings on a page is a thought process you do. So carefully and slowly look inside yourself and discover how you engaged in the behavior of giving meaning to each of these markings on the page. Take your time. The rest of the book will wait.

If you were very attentive, you'll notice that you had an internal re-presentation triggered in response to these words. Some saw something. Others heard something. Others felt something.

Perhaps some even smelled something (as Greg did with the word *vomit*). Even among those who, for instance, saw things in their minds, what they saw was different for each person. Al's *elephant* was slightly different from your *elephant*. Greg's *vomit* was different from your *vomit*.

As some transformational linguists put it, the *surface structure meaning* of our words was the same for all of us, but the *deep structure* of these words—the actual mental behavior we each did to retrieve the meaning of these words—was different for each of us.[6] The shared *surface meaning* is what makes communication possible, but the differing *deep structure* is what makes it difficult.

A man proudly tells his wife, "I'm making dinner tonight." She assumes he remembered her birthday and is delighted. She's picturing (and maybe tasting and smelling) a steak, vegetables, mashed potatoes, and a nice wine. In reality, however, the husband didn't remember her birthday at all. He just doesn't want to wait for dinner because it might cut into his Monday night football game. So he's imagining himself "cooking" a frozen pizza, drinking a Pepsi, and then kicking back with some buddies to watch a good game. Same surface meaning; very different deep structure.

What's important for us right now is to simply realize we have a deep structure to our thoughts. Indeed, this deep structure is the essence of our thoughts. We communicate with surface structure meaning, providing verbal information to others. But our thoughts have their own VAKOG structure that cannot be communicated.

The neurologically generated virtual reality prison that kept humans enslaved in the movie *The Matrix* wasn't far off from what is happening to us in the "pattern" of our world (Rom. 12:1–2). For lies that keep us in bondage are not on the surface, contained in conceptual information. They are rooted deep within us and are experientially re-presented under the right external triggers.

Conceptual Information and Internal Experience

Most of us haven't paid attention to Aristotle's insight that "the soul never thinks without images." Most people just assume they think with conceptual information—which perhaps explains why we tend to trust conceptual information so much to transform us, despite our uniform experience that this trust doesn't usually pay off. We just haven't known there was anything else to go on. Why have we missed this?

Think of it this way. If we asked you to describe an elephant, you can only give us conceptual information. You'd say something like, "A very large mammal with a long trunk." You'd give us our shared surface structure meaning, not your deep structure meaning. But it's not because you want to hide anything from us. It's simply that you can't possibly give us your deep structure—that is, what you're actually *experiencing* when you do the behavior of "thinking of an elephant."

Only *you* can experience your actual mental behavior. Only *you* can experience your neural-nets from the inside. Only *you* can see, hear, and sense what you *do* in your mind. Only *you* have direct access to your deep structure. To give *others* an answer, you have to provide an informational report of what you experience. And you have to use the shared surface meaning of words to do it. So you abstract conceptual information *out from* your internal experience to communicate to others. You give interpretive *information about* your thought because you simply can't give the internal holographic experience that *is* your thought.

Because the holographic virtual reality we experience in our minds occurs much faster than our ordinary, conscious minds notice, and because we are so used to instantly producing this virtual reality under the right triggers (asking a question, for example, triggers a search for meaning), we usually assume that the *information* we *give* is *the reality we experienced*. We mistake the abstracted information for the actual internal experience. In fact, because we rarely if ever need to become conscious of our mental images in daily life, many people don't even know they have them. We think we "just know" things. In reality, however, we know things because we experience them inside. Or better, our real knowing is an experience—a sensory experience in our minds.

Remember, your brain only gives your conscious mind five to nine chunks of the 2 million pieces of information it is processing each second in accordance with whatever it deems relevant for a task it is performing. Our odd questions through this chapter have (hopefully) been forcing your brain to make your mental images relevant to your conscious mind. But in ordinary life our brains don't deem this information relevant, which is why it's so easy to miss. It's also a major reason why we stay enslaved in the Matrix. We can consciously know a good deal of true information while unconsciously experiencing lies. And experience almost always trumps conceptual information.

If we are going to take every thought captive to Christ, we're going to have to do so according to the rules that govern thought. And the rule is: thought is a form of experience, and the more concrete and like reality the experience, the more impact it has on you.[7] You can't fight experiential cancer with a Band-Aid of conceptual information.

Virtual Reality Neurochips

In the last chapter we likened a neural-net to a microchip implanted in the brain, which we're calling a "neurochip." Let's re-investigate Doreen's neurochip in the light of what we've learned about the nature of thought in this chapter.

Remember, what actually happened was that a handful of grasshoppers were put down the back of Doreen's shirt. Doreen didn't actually see the insects that were on her back, and feeling what was crawling under her shirt activated Doreen's creative imagination and exacerbated the incident far beyond reality. A few grasshoppers turned into hundreds of flesh-eating, slimy, ugly little monsters crawling all over her body.

The neurochip in Doreen's brain that triggered her fear of insects did more than just give her wrong conceptual information. The adult Doreen knew all the right information. She knew that with rare exceptions insects are not dangerous and that steering clear of the rare dangerous ones is relatively easy. But once activated, the neurochip that was installed when Doreen was nine had the power to override all this information. Why? Because it did much more than give misinformation; it vividly re-presented an experience that embodied misinformation.

At the sight of an insect, or even at the possibility of coming into contact with an insect, a thirty-year-old neural-net was activated. It was for all intents and purposes the same neural-net that thirty years earlier was formed by interpreting Doreen's sensation of waking up to bugs crawling under her shirt. It was the same neural-net that embodied the emotion of a nine-year-old's terror of being eaten alive.

Once the neural-net was activated, Doreen entered into a virtual reality in which she felt the insects on her eyes and mouth, crawling in her hair, slithering on her stomach. She was "making present again"—re-presenting—her nine-year-old experience from the same perspective she had when the neural-net was first installed. Upon the right trigger, she entered the Matrix. As an adult, Doreen was not conscious of the virtual reality she entered, for it happened in a fraction of a second, far faster than her conscious mind could capture. But she *felt* its impact. The memory flashes for a millisecond and is gone, leaving behind a terrorized little girl who is now thirty-nine years old.

This is perhaps the most sinister aspect of the Matrix. Doreen's amazing brain was efficiently doing its job, operating with its God-given design, but it was being used against her. Her brain was trying to protect her by responding to triggers and immediately recalling past experiences that might be significant to her present experiences. This is how the brain tells us that something is *good* or *bad*. And it is so efficient at doing this that it usually tells us this before we are consciously aware of anything *good* or *bad*.

In a fallen world in bondage to the god of this age, the brain often installs lies instead of truth. This is how the Matrix is constructed. If the brain experientially concludes insects are life-threatening, carnivorous beasts, it sticks with it. This becomes part of its autopilot. Under the right circumstances—the right triggers—it reproduces the experience, employing all the relevant senses, using just the right VAKOG code, embodying all the relevant emotions.[8] Beneath the radar of Doreen's conscious mind, the insects are seen, heard, and felt from the perspective of a terrorized nine-year-old. The past is made present again, and the result is significant bondage to a lie that she will be devoured by insects.

How could a thirty-nine-year-old, intelligent, successful woman have a panic attack at the sight of a spider? *This* is how.

. . . .
The Power of a Matrix Neurochip

The efficiency with which our brains can re-present lies is how we all stay conformed to and in bondage to the Matrix of this world. The power of thought lies in the experiential vividness of what it re-presents. Consider a few more real-life examples.

———— ∽∽∾ ————

A six-year-old boy is helping his father put up a swing set in the backyard. The boy is excited as the set is being erected, and he's enjoying the bonding experience of working on something important with his father. At one point the father asks his son to hand him the socket wrench. Not knowing what a socket wrench is but earnestly wanting to help his father, the boy hands him a pair of small pliers. The father, perhaps already frustrated from trying to put the swing set together, remarks in frustration, "You're as useless as tits on a boar."

A neurochip is installed. The boy doesn't know what a "boar" is or what "tits" are, but he doesn't need to. He knows he is useless and stupid. Dad said so, and with a tone and volume that registered this meaning in the boy. His six-year-old brain then engages in some Matrix reasoning. He concludes that making mistakes is not about learning but about broadcasting how useless and stupid he really is. One must therefore always appear competent, right, and useful.

This is an exquisite example of the Architect's strategy. It's a classic Catch-22. The devil convinces a person of a lie and then convinces him or her of the need to hide the lie at all costs. When lies like this are installed, we spend a significant portion of our lives trying *not* to be what we never were in the first place!

Forty years later, despite his adult knowledge that his worth is found in Christ, the boy experiences the shame of this episode over and over again. Under certain circumstances, and at a fraction of a second, he sees his father's face, hears his frustrated words, and feels a six-year-old's shame. The adult is unconscious of the neurochip-activated reality that instantly takes place in his brain, *but he feels its impact*. Not surprisingly, the adult is compulsive about never making mistakes, proving that he is smart and always right, and trying to make himself important to others.

A little boy is still trying to disprove a thoughtless expression of a frustrated father. A peaceful child of God, who has been given worth and freedom in Christ, has been robotically reduced to a defensive, argumentative overachiever by a Matrix neurochip.

———

A seventeen-year-old woman gets pregnant, panics, and has an abortion. A neurochip is installed. Thirty-five years later, despite her knowledge that God has forgiven her and that she is holy and blameless in Christ, the woman continues to vividly re-experience the abortion. Under the right conditions, she instantly re-presents the same panic and inner conflict she felt then. She sees her spread legs in stirrups and sees and hears the doctor trying to be nonchalant about the matter. She feels and hears the suctioning abortion device. She smells the clinical odor of the doctor's office. She experiences the same shame and grief she experienced then. The same neurochip is activated.

The fifty-two-year-old lady consciously believes the true information that she has been told that her abortion is forgiven. And she consciously thinks she's put it all behind her. So she's puzzled as to why she has been dogged all her life with a feeling that she doesn't quite measure up and is not lovable.

A teenage girl is still being flogged for a sin long since forgiven. A redeemed child of God who has been given God's holiness and joy has been robotically reduced to a sad, shame-filled woman by a Matrix neurochip.

———

A ten-year-old girl is repeatedly molested by her older brother. With God-given efficiency, her brain installs the events with the interpretation that sex is dirty, painful, and dangerous. A neurochip has been installed.

Twelve years later the woman is married but discovers she doesn't enjoy sexual relations with her husband. When I (Al) asked her to describe her feelings about sex, her response was "icky"—a little girl's word for "revolting" (helping me understand that her perspective on sex is *still* that of a traumatized young girl). Though the adult woman believes the true information that sex is a beautiful, safe, and positive aspect of marriage, she emotionally freezes whenever her husband tries to initiate sex. The trigger of his advances activates a virtual reality replication of the molestation, and she experiences it anew—but from the same ten-year-old perspective and with the same ten-year-old feelings she had when it occurred. She continued to be plagued with the same mistaken ten-year-old conclusion about sex.

A young girl continued to suffer from a history far behind her. Her brain had installed the conclusion that "sex was icky" as part of its autopilot. Hence, a precious child of God who should have been experiencing an intimacy and ecstasy with her husband that mirrors God's own being (Eph. 5:25–32) had been robotically reduced to an emotionally frozen spouse by a Matrix neurochip.

Often it's innocuous, random events, rather than people, that install neurochips in us. A five-year-old boy is watching the evening news with his dad. A report comes on about a plane crash. It briefly shows the demolished, burning plane followed by a quick view of some body bags and a report of the number of people who were killed. Ten thousand kids could see this report and have nothing happen. But for reasons too complex for us to discern, this young boy's brain concludes that planes must be avoided at all costs. His brain is just trying to do its job and keep him safe.

Twenty-six years later a man is terrified of flying and has no idea why. He hasn't once thought about the news program he saw as a child. But he's thought a lot about planes! He knows all the right information about how safe they are. He is certain about his salvation and knows physical death is temporary. As with all phobias, his fear reaction is irrational. But it makes perfect sense to the five-year-old perspective of the neurochip that gets activated every time he thinks about flying. His brain instantaneously replicates a five-year-old's experience of imagining himself on that crashing plane and replicates the five-year-old's misinformed conclusion.

A child of God who has been given a fearless spirit has been robotically reduced to a person governed by fears by a Matrix neurochip.

Who Controls the Life?

Every single aspect of our emotions and behavior that do not conform to the truth of who we are in Christ is due to a Matrix neurochip. Under the right triggers, we vividly experience as real things that are not real. With all five senses we mentally experience lies as though they were truth. The neurologically generated virtual world of our minds is out of sync with the real world. Hence our actual experience of ourselves—and of God and our world—is out of sync with truth. Consequently, our emotions and behaviors are out of sync with the emotions and behaviors that could and should characterize a healthy human being, let alone a Spirit-filled child of God.

To the extent that we have Matrix neurochips in our brains, we are robots in service to whomever and whatever programmed and installed the neurochips. Consciously, we think we are free, but to this degree we are not. For remember: whoever controls the neurons controls the life.

If we're going to be set free, we've got to become vigilant detectives of our minds, locating and eradicating the Matrix neurochips in our brains.

Exercise 3

Discovering the Modalities of Memory

The purpose of this exercise is to help you begin to become aware of the virtual reality in your mind that you experience when you think. More specifically, we want you to discover the modality and submodality distinctions you do when producing various re-presentations associated to various emotions. This exercise will help you begin to discover how you uniquely structure your thought to elicit particular emotions. It will help you become a more effective detective of your mind.

What follows is a series of questions we want you to answer as you hold a memory vividly in mind. Our questions fall into three categories that correspond to the main three senses (modalities) people normally employ in thought. The first set of questions is about what and how you see (visual modality). The second is about what and how you hear (auditory modality). And the third is about what and how you feel or sense things in your memory (kinesthetic modality).

We want you to apply these categories to four different memories: a pleasant memory, a memory of being angry, a memory of being frightened, and a memory of being sad. You should pause and think about something else after each memory you investigate. (We call this a "pattern interrupt.")[9] It's necessary to clear away a thought to allow for a new thought to occur. If this is not done, feelings from one memory may bleed over into another and hinder your investigation.) After answering the question for each of the four memories, we want you to compare the different ways you do the submodality distinctions in each of the differing memories.

We strongly recommend you write down your answers to each question. Do not simply answer yes or no. Rather, explain each answer. For example, if you see color, describe what colors you see. You should note that not all questions will necessarily apply to each memory. For example, some people may not see anything in their memory of being afraid. If you are such a person, all the questions pertaining to the submodality distinctions of the visual modality will be left blank when it comes to your memory of being afraid.

Finally, you should know that this is only a partial list of the modality and submodality distinctions that are possible. Feel free to record other aspects of your memories that seem relevant to the emotion of the memory.

Now, recall as vividly as possible a pleasant memory. Then *pattern interrupt* yourself (that is, pause, say with a loud internal voice, "STOP NOW," and think about breakfast tomorrow or something else), and then recall as vividly as possible a memory of being angry. Do the same for a memory of being afraid and a memory of being sad.

Answer the following questions with regard to each of these memories.

Visual Modality: What do you **see** in doing a memory?

1. *Do you see your memory in color, or is it in black and white?*

   Pleasant memory   *Colour .*

   Angry memory

   Fearful memory   *B/w .*

   Sad memory   *Colour .*

   What stands out when you compare how you do each of these memories?

   The pleasant memory was easier to focus on .

2. *Do you see yourself (your body) in the memory (disassociated), or do you see it through your own eyes (associated)?*

   Pleasant memory   *own eyes*

   Angry memory   *" 7*

   Fearful memory   *" 7*

   Sad memory   *" "*

   What stands out when you compare how you do each of these memories?

   in in how of makes me feel (emotions)

3. *Is there movement in your memory (like a video), or is it a still frame (like a photograph)?*

Pleasant memory   *Moving*

Angry memory

Fearful memory   ᴧ

Sad memory   ᴧ

What stands out when you compare how you do each of these memories?   *emohons*

4. *Is your memory relatively bright or relatively dim?*

Pleasant memory   *quite dim* -

Angry memory   ᴧ

Fearful memory   ᴧ

Sad memory   ᴧ

What stands out when you compare how you do each of these memories?

5. *Is your memory three-dimensional or two-dimensional?*

Pleasant memory   *Three* ·

Angry memory

Fearful memory   ᴧ

Sad memory   ᴧ

What stands out when you compare how you do each of these memories?

- - - - - - - - - - - - - - - - - -

Auditory Modality: What do you **hear** in doing a memory?

1. *Do you hear words or sounds in your memory? If so, what are they?*

   Pleasant memory   Sounds like reliving it.

   Angry memory

   Fearful memory   ⌐

   Sad memory   ⌐

   What stands out when you compare how you do each of these memories?

2. *If you hear words, are they in your voice or someone else's? If you hear someone else's voice, whose is it?*

   Pleasant memory   Me ˌ

   Angry memory

   Fearful memory

   Sad memory   Me .

   What stands out when you compare how you do each of these memories?

3. *What is the texture of the voice and/or sounds you hear? (For example, is it soft or loud, gentle or harsh, etc.?)*

Pleasant memory   *Same as orginal Memorh.*

Angry memory

Fearful memory   *y*

Sad memory   *M*

What stands out when you compare how you do each of these memories?

4. *Is the speed of the voice and/or sounds slow, normal, or fast?*

Pleasant memory

Angry memory

Fearful memory

Sad memory

What stands out when you compare how you do each of these memories?

5. *Is there a location of the voice and/or sounds (e.g., are they coming from someone or somewhere in the memory), or are they panoramic, like surround sound?*

Pleasant memory   *Memorh*

Angry memory

Fearful memory

Sad memory

What stands out when you compare how you do each of these memories?

Kinesthetic Modality: What do you **feel** in doing a memory?

1. *Is there any physical feeling associated with this memory (e.g., a cool breeze, warm sun)?* *No* ,

   Pleasant memory

   Angry memory

   Fearful memory

   Sad memory

   What stands out when you compare how you do each of these memories?

2. *Is there anything you smell or taste in this memory?*

   Pleasant memory

   Angry memory   *No*

   Fearful memory

   Sad memory

   What stands out when you compare how you do each of these memories?

3. *What emotions are associated with this memory? Label them.*

Pleasant memory *Joy, happyness.*

Angry memory

Fearful memory *fear*

Sad memory *Sad, alone. loss.*

What stands out when you compare how you do each of these memories?

4. *How intense are the emotions associated with the memory? Rate them on a scale of 1 (very low) to 10 (very high).*

Pleasant memory *8*

Angry memory

Fearful memory *6*

Sad memory *9.*

What stands out when you compare how you do each of these memories?

5. *Do the emotions associated with the memory seem to be located in a place in your body (for example, in your chest, stomach, head, or legs)?*

Pleasant memory *head.*

Angry memory

Fearful memory *stomach.*

Sad memory *heart*

What stands out when you compare how you do each of these memories?

6. *Does your memory feel soft or hard, smooth or rough, or another texture?*

Pleasant memory   *Soft*.

Angry memory

Fearful memory   *heaver*.

Sad memory   *disconnected*.

What stands out when you compare how you do each of these memories?

We recommend that you carry out this exercise at different times in relation to a different set of pleasant, angry, fearful, and sad memories. In all of this, you are learning to become conscious of an inner world most humans are rarely conscious of—a world that often imprisons us for this very reason. It is the virtual-reality world of our minds. As we become aware of the way we do various types of thoughts and emotions, we become empowered to choose different ways of doing the various types. And this, we shall see, is the key to escaping the Matrix and setting the mind free to experience real life in Christ.

4

Waging War within the Matrix

Learning How to Take Thoughts Captive

MORPHEUS: Men have emptied entire clips at [agents] and hit nothing but air. Yet their strength and their speed are still based in a world that is built on rules. Because of that, they will never be as strong or as fast as you can be.

⸙

For though we live in the world, we do not wage war as the world does. The weapons we fight with are not the weapons of the world. On the contrary, they have divine power to demolish strongholds. We demolish arguments and every pretension that sets itself up against the knowledge of God, and we take captive every thought to make it obedient to Christ.

2 Corinthians 10:3–5

Watch over your heart with all diligence, for from it flow the springs of life.

Proverbs 4:23 NASB

It's *Your* Organic Computer

God didn't create you to be imprisoned in your mind and a slave to forces outside yourself. God created you to be free, Jesus died to set you free, and the Spirit now works in your life to empower you to be free. Whatever it is that presently holds you in bondage, it doesn't have to be there. You can experience real life—free life—in Jesus Christ!

This brings us to the single most important part of our exploration of the Matrix. As subtle as it is, as fast as it is, as experiential as it is, and as powerful as it is, the Matrix *is not unalterable*. You are not condemned to the status of a Matrix-controlled robot. Through Christ, empowered by the Spirit, and working in accordance with God's design for the brain, we can penetrate the Matrix, tear it down, and destroy it (2 Cor. 10:3–5).

We want you to see something that is at once very simple and extremely important. We'll do this by having you go through yet another one of our rather strange but very revealing exercises. This exercise will help you learn further how the brain structures internal experience.

Remember the elephant you thought about in the last chapter? Well, think about it again. Imagine it as vividly as you are able. Take whatever time you need to do this.

Now some of you can see this elephant vividly and can hold it in focus indefinitely. Others may see it clearly at first but can't seem to keep it in focus. Still others may have difficulty seeing the elephant at all. You have an impression of an elephant. You feel it's there, but you don't distinctly see it. This is all well and good. People re-present ideas in their minds in unique ways.

However you re-present the elephant, we want you to discover that you have the power to alter this re-presentation. So, if your elephant is standing still, we want you to have it start walking. If it was already walking, we want you to make it stand still.

Now have it stand on its hind legs, like a circus elephant doing a trick. Once this is done, add some sound to the image by having your elephant let out a loud elephant roar. Can you hear it? Now have him take off into the air and start flying with his ears, like Dumbo.

Okay, freeze-frame your flying elephant and put borders around your vision of it. Re-present it as a still-frame picture.

Now shrink it into a photograph. Hold the photograph in your hand. Put some clouds in the background of the flying elephant in the photograph. A bird or two around the elephant would be nice as well. Got it?

Finally, put a match to the bottom of the photograph and watch it burn from the bottom up.

What, you might ask, is the point of this odd exercise? Simply this: *You have power over your thoughts!* As we have said, we do not produce thoughts as pieces of information. We rather re-present reality in the form of things we see, hear, and sense on the inside. These re-presentations are what give our thoughts their emotional charge, which in turn stimulate our behavior. While we cannot directly alter our emotions at will, we *can* alter the re-presentations that ground our emotions and thereby gain power over our behavior.

The bottom line is that you can make your brain do whatever you want, as our above exercise demonstrated. This may be difficult at first, especially for people who have never taken control of their thoughts before. But the truth is that your brain is wired to be told what to do—if not by you, then by people and forces other than you. But God wants *you* to be your brain's primary programmer. It's *your* tool to interface with reality and it's *your* responsibility to keep it running well. Scripture commands *you* to guard your thoughts and emotions, to take thoughts captive, and to renew your mind (Prov. 4:23; Rom. 12:2; 2 Cor. 10:3–5; Eph. 4:22–24).

Of course it's also true that God created us as social creatures who mutually define one another, so parents, friends, and other influences in the outside world are also intended to impact our brains. Were the world not fallen, these outside influences would serve to reinforce our perception of truth. We would help one another experience reality "on the inside" the way reality actually is. Our interactions with each other would replicate God's loving interactions with us. Our thoughts and emotions would therefore be completely congruent with truth as defined by God. This is how it shall be when God's kingdom has fully come. When this happens, God's loving rule shall define the whole of reality.

In the meantime, however, the world continues to exist under a strong, oppressive influence from Satan. In this oppressed state, outside influences communicate and reinforce lies in our minds as often as they do truth. This is how the Matrix is constructed. And this is what makes our individual role in guarding our thoughts and emotions so important.

We still desperately need people around us who install and reinforce truth in our minds, which is one of the reasons Scripture places such importance on living in community within the body of Christ. But ultimately, the responsibility for rooting out Matrix neurochips and installing truth in our minds rests with us as individuals and our obedience to God's Word and the Spirit who indwells us.

Living as a Resurrected Neo

Though most (but not all) neuroscience today assumes that humans are reducible to their deterministic neurological activity, Scripture, as well as our own experience, tells us otherwise.[2] Though we (unfortunately) may not exercise it often, we have the power to control our thoughts and therefore our emotions. Were this not so, the multitude of scriptural commands to control our thoughts and emotions would be meaningless (see Prov. 4:23; Rom. 12:2; 2 Cor. 10:5; Eph. 4:22–23; Phil. 4:8; Heb. 4:12). Above all, we are to think about ourselves as we are in Christ, not as we are defined by "the pattern of this world" (Rom. 6:11). The whole business of sanctification is contained in these commands. It's not about struggling to change our emotions or behavior by our own will power. It's about dying to the lie of the Matrix and getting our thoughts to line up with reality!

The extent to which we do this is the extent to which we successfully wage war within the Matrix. The point is powerfully illustrated toward the end of *The Matrix*. Neo had been killed by the agents of the Matrix but is resurrected by Trinity's faith and love. It is only at this time that Neo finally believes the truth and experiences the reality that he has power over the agents of the Matrix. He has died to the Matrix and has let go of all fear, doubt, and disbelief. His mind has been freed. He now believes Morpheus's teaching that the agents can never be as strong or as fast as he. He finally lives up to his name—Neo (meaning "new"). Finally, Mr. Anderson (Neo) is in fact a "new creation" (2 Cor. 5:17).

From this time on, the battle within the Matrix will be fought in a new way. Neo now fights from a position of victor to help others break free from the Matrix. In the words of agent Smith, Neo's own freedom from the Matrix as well as the freedom of all who will choose to follow him is "inevitable."

So it is with us. We have in fact been resurrected by the Trinity. Our real identity is found in Christ. We truly are *new* creations. When we finally put aside all fear, doubt, and disbelief and fully accept this fact—despite all our experiences to the contrary—we are empowered to extinguish the "agents" of the Matrix—what we've been calling "Matrix neurochips." We no longer futilely fight to *gain* an identity we think we don't yet have. Instead we realize our identity is already established in Christ. We wake up to the fact that we are exhaustively defined by Christ's death and resurrection. Thus, our battle within the Matrix is not to *establish* the truth of who we are but to *apply* the truth of who we are to all our thoughts, emotions, and behavior. And we understand that our total conformity to Christ is a matter of inevitability. From before creation it was predestined that all who chose to trust in Christ would ultimately be "holy and blameless in [God's] sight" (Eph. 1:4; see Rom. 8:29).

As people who have been set free by Christ, we are to consider ourselves free in Christ (Rom. 6:11). We are to wage war within the Matrix from a position of strength, not weakness. We are to know that, as influential as the Architect of the Matrix is in this world, the one at work in us is far greater (1 John 4:4). Knowing who we are, knowing to whom we belong, knowing who indwells us, knowing our birthright, and knowing our ultimate destiny, we are to take charge of our thoughts and emotions and bring every one of them into alignment with truth.

The extent to which we do this is the extent to which our minds dwell on what is true, noble, right, pure, lovely, admirable, excellent, and praiseworthy (Phil. 4:8). It is the extent to which we internally *experience* truth rather than simply *know about* truth theoretically.

Cooperating with God for a Change®

It's all about debugging your brain of Matrix neurochips. You can learn as much as you are capable of learning, but if your neural-nets aren't altered, if the renegade neurochips are left installed, it will change nothing about you. You can strive as much as you have energy to strive, but if you don't change what you automatically see, hear, and sense in your mind when certain triggers are activated, you won't be transformed. In fact, though this may offend some, you can pray as much as you can possibly pray and fast as much as your body will take, but even these praiseworthy activities won't free you from the Matrix except insofar as they empower you to *take thoughts captive*. For your whole sense of reality is contained in the neurological firings within the organic computer between your ears.

Both in pastoral ministry and in counseling we've encountered people who say they are just "waiting on God" to change them. They are completely passive concerning the ungodly thoughts, attitudes, emotions, and behaviors in their lives. Some have been taught this is all one can do, and they honestly feel spiritual for doing it.

Now, we are the first to insist that we are not able to do anything without Christ empowering us (John 15:4–5). But we're also the first to insist that, with rare miraculous exceptions, God doesn't unilaterally change our brains without our cooperation. It is unwise, unbiblical, and frankly irresponsible for people to do nothing while they passively wait on God to change them. God is *already* at work in their lives to change them. *He's* the one waiting on *them*!

As with Neo, others can perhaps show you the door to freedom, but as Morpheus says, "You're the one that has to walk through it." You have a crucial role to play in getting free from the Matrix.

Scripture teaches that we are to "work out [not work *at*] your salvation" knowing that "it is God who works in you" (Phil. 2:12–13). God is at work in and through *our work* to manifest the freedom and abundant life we have in Christ. But this assumes that we do in fact work!

Think of it this way. God doesn't want to do what Satan has always been trying to do: namely, reduce us to automated robots. On the contrary, God is working in us and through us to free us from a robotic existence—which is why he works in and through *our working*. He created us to be free, and we must freely choose to work with him to be liberated from every neurochip that keeps us in bondage.

The central role we play in spiritual growth and the central area of our warfare is not in working to change our *bodily* behavior but in *cooperating* with God to change our *mental* behavior. Our bodily behavior is never more than a symptom. Trying to change bodily behavior while leaving the brain unchanged is another form of treating cancer with a Band-Aid.

The primary warfare in which we are called to be involved lies in the brain. We are commissioned to take back what the enemy stole from us: our minds. Hence Scripture teaches that we are transformed by *renewing our minds*. God is at work in us to reinstate us as the rightful owners and authorities over our brains. He is working in us and through us to debug our brains of Matrix neurochips and to align our brains with truth.

The only questions are: Will you work with him to see this accomplished? Will you make a decision to cooperate with God for a change?[1]

God's Design and Satan's Design

Scripture tells us that we are not to be ignorant of Satan's schemes (2 Cor. 2:11). Sadly, there are few schemes of the devil that we tend to be more ignorant of than the one he uses to keep us enslaved in the Matrix.

Be honest. Prior to doing the exercises in chapters 2 and 3, did you often give serious thought to what you think about? Even more to the point, did you often give serious thought to *the way you actually think about things*—the actual images, words, and impressions that constitute your moment-by-moment thought world?

Like the imprisoned people in the movie *The Matrix*, most people are so completely immersed in the Matrix that they don't even know there's a Matrix. Being unaware of how their neural-nets are controlled, they just assume their neural-nets accurately convey reality. They assume that their cognitive (neurological) map of the world is the real world. But it's not.

Believing that everything that feels real is true is what keeps us imprisoned. The Architect is using the God-given efficiency of our brains to keep us duped. What God intended for good, the enemy uses for evil.

It will help to spell out our situation in a bit more detail.

God's Original Design

Lord
↓
Spirit
↓
Mind
↓
Body
↓
World
↓
Satan

In God's design, the core of our being—our "spirit" (Heb. 4:12)—is to be submitted to him. God is to be the ultimate authority telling us as spirit-beings who we are. We are then to have authority over our minds, which includes our thoughts and emotions.[3] Our minds are then to have authority over our bodies, telling them to act out the truths we believe. And through our bodies we are to have authority over our physical environment. We were created to have dominion over the earth (Gen. 1:26–28). We are to be partners with God's loving lordship and are to work with God to see his will done "on earth as it is in heaven" (Matt. 6:10).

Satan's Design

Spirit
↑
Mind
↑
Body
↑
World
↑
Satan

The god of this age seeks to reverse God's wonderful arrangement, and he's largely successful in this fallen world. Satan literally "perverts" it (from the Latin *perversio,* meaning "to turn upside down"). He uses the world to impact our bodies—all that we experience with our senses—to lie to our minds about what is true. And our spirits submit to this! "That's just the way I am," or, "That's just the way I see things," we often hear people say. And God is basically out of the picture. Sadly, such people are immersed in the Matrix.

We might say that whereas God's design has us defined from the *top down* (God → spirit) and from the *inside out* (spirit → mind → body → world), Satan attempts to define us from the *bottom up* (Satan → world) and from the *outside in* (world → body → mind → spirit). He wants us to be merely robotic extensions of the people and events we've experienced and thereby conformed to the pattern of the world he is over.

Now when we in our innermost being ("spirit") are submitted to God, the proper order of things is restored in terms of the God → spirit relationship. The spirit of the regenerate person genuinely wants to live in relationship with God and to do his will. All that God says is true about us in Scripture *is* true on this level. We are in our innermost being identified with Christ and are holy, blameless, filled with all the fullness of God, etc. But the proper spirit → mind relationship is not automatically restored. On the contrary, because they are rooted in our physical neural-nets, our thoughts and emotions continue on in their autopilot fashion, however they've been programmed to run, for good or for ill. This is why we don't automatically *experience* the truth of who we truly are in Christ.

The reason God doesn't give us a spiritual lobotomy the moment we believe is that God wants *us* to reacquire the authority he originally gave us. Remember, he created us to have dominion over the earth. He wants us to freely choose to be the administrators of his loving providence. His ultimate aim is to have a bride who freely chooses to receive and give back his love and who, out of the fullness of love and life she receives from him, reigns with him upon the earth (2 Tim. 2:12; Rev. 5:10).

In other words, we are created and saved to be nothing less than corulers over all the earth! God wants us to work with him to dethrone the one who presently controls the world (1 John 5:19) and take back what he stole. Once we are regenerated by the Spirit of God, the first "plot of land" God commands us to take back, if you will, is the area between our ears—our brains.

Indeed, taking back this plot of land is the precondition for taking back anything else. For only to the extent that our minds are aligned with God will our behavior be aligned with God. And only then can we hope to bring the world into alignment with God through our behavior.

If our life mission is to see God's kingdom come "on earth as it is in heaven" (Matt. 6:10), we must concentrate most strongly on seeing God's kingdom come in our minds as it is in heaven. The gap between our regenerate spirits and our largely unregenerate minds explains why we can genuinely want to do God's will in the core of our being and yet find that we experience desires, motivations, emotions, and behaviors that are completely out of sync with God's will. We are defined by the top down in terms of the God → spirit relationship the moment we truly surrender to Christ. But we are still largely defined from the bottom up in body → soul → spirit relationship.

The Warfare of the Redeemed Person

Lord
↓
Spirit
↓
Warzone
for the Mind
↑
Body
↑
Satan

This also explains why the New Testament locates the central place of spiritual warfare in the mind. *It is here that God's design and Satan's design most directly clash.* Christ is at work in us, empowering us to bring about our liberation in the mind. But *we* must assert our God-given authority over our brains and work with him to experience this liberation. To do this effectively, we must work in accordance with the way he designed our brains to operate.

Experience Installs Neurochips

Why have many of us been largely unsuccessful in taking back most of the "plot of land" between our ears? The most basic answer, we believe, is that we have tended to trust information too much and ignored how the brain actually works. These are two sides of the same coin.

Morpheus couldn't just give information to Neo about the Matrix. Neo had to experience it for himself.

If you want to learn how the brain works, pay attention to the ones who get paid the most to influence it—advertisers. You're watching Monday night football and a commercial comes on. A pensive young man (the target audience) holding a bottle of beer knocks on the door. A gorgeous, seductive young lady answers. (They have the target audience's attention!) She's been painting her apartment and is obviously hot and thirsty. She's wearing only a loose shirt that barely goes down past her hips. She stares at him with sensuous, inviting eyes.

The "target audience" has forgotten all about the game.

A montage of graphic scenes quickly follow, accompanied by catchy music and a pulsating beat. We see the man's hand vigorously shaking the beer by its neck, creating foam in the bottle. Next we see the woman reaching up as she's painting, almost exposing her buttocks. A close-up of her face reveals an expression that could be interpreted as either intense ecstasy or pain—or both.

Next shot: the window of her apartment viewed from the outside. Suddenly a ton of *snow* blasts out of the window into the hot summer air!

Final scene: the man and woman are sitting on the floor of the apartment looking very relaxed as they enjoy a refreshing beer. A logo for the brand of beer that paid for all this comes on the screen.

That's it. Freud would have been proud.

The question we need to ask is: what on earth do any of these outrageous scenes have to do with the brand of beer being advertised—or any beer for that matter? And the answer, of course, is *absolutely nothing*. But *that is clearly beside the point.*

The aim of this and most other commercials is not primarily to give information about the product. After all, in terms of information, there is little positive correlation between beer and sex. In fact, if there's any real-life correlation at all, it's negative. How many gorgeous young women do you know who are attracted to guys with beer breath and beer bellies? And how many men find that drinking beer enhances their sex drive? You see our point.

But that's not *their* point. Information is pretty much irrelevant. The aim of their commercial is to give their target audience (young men) an experience they'll henceforth unconsciously associate with the product. They're trying to install neurochips!

Advertisers get paid millions of dollars to know how the brain works. What they know and ingeniously utilize to their advantage is something the church desperately needs to learn (Luke 16:8). The brain thinks by imaginatively reexperiencing things when triggered to do so. The closer the brain's images are to real life, the stronger we feel the emotions associated with them and the more these emotions affect our behavior. Hence, the more vivid, concrete, and startling the advertisements, the more likely they are to be vividly remembered and associated with the product. In other words, the more likely they are to motivate us to purchase what they're selling.

In the case of the commercial cited above, the advertisers clearly hope that a young man's sexual feelings—or his desire for beer—will activate the vivid sexual images of their commercial and thus be associated with their brand of beer. The subjects, of course, won't be conscious of the experiential images activated in their minds, for these occur far faster than our ordinary conscious thought can detect. *That's largely why they work.* But if the commercial has been successful, the subjects will subtly *feel* and *act on* the impact of these images. Young men will simply *find themselves* wanting this particular brand of beer. And as far as their conscious minds know, it has got nothing to do with getting a gorgeous girl.

But the advertisers know better. They know that what you *consciously believe* impacts and transforms you much less than what you *actually experience* in your mind.

The Matrix of the world is so powerful in conforming us to itself because it controls our experience of the world, even when it doesn't control our information—indeed, even when our information runs directly counter to our experience.

■ ■
Theology and Beer Commercials

If you've ever wondered why we modern Western Christians can know so much about the Bible and theology and yet experience so little transformation, we believe you've just found your answer. All our lives we are impacted with experiences and are given messages that are real, experiential, vivid, and sometimes startling:

> waking up with grasshoppers down your shirt when you're nine
> hearing your father tell you that you're useless
> being molested by an older brother
> having your father ask an older bully to beat you up
> experiencing vivid images linking beer with sex

Consider the multitude of vivid experiences you've had that do not communicate the truth of God's will for your life. Think of the thousands upon thousands of commercials we see on television, billboards, and magazines. Think of the millions of scenes from television shows and movies we watch. Consider the suggestive songs we repeatedly hear on the radio as well as the graphic stories some of us read. All of these impact us through our senses and are re-presented in our minds when triggered. They each communicate assumptions about reality, about what "the good life" is, about what values we should embrace, about our worth and value (or lack of it). All of these messages thus influence how we are inclined to act. But when assessed by the criteria of what the Creator says is true, many of these messages must be judged as lies.

To the extent our neurological sense of reality is formed by lies such as these, we are defined from the bottom up and the outside in. We are trapped in the Matrix.

How are we equipped to battle all of this? For the most part, we are given information and moral encouragements. We are told, "You need to know this and that," and, "You ought to do such and such." This information and encouragement isn't bad, mind you. But it is not transforming. Our theology may be entirely correct and the moral instruction we receive absolutely sound, but neither can compete with graphic images of a seductive beer commercial because the vivid commercials operate more in accord with how the brain actually works than do our theological information and moral instruction.

It's simply a fact that we're neurologically wired to be impacted by what we experience as real, by experiences and internal images that are seen, heard, and felt. Memories have power because they speak this language. Commercials have power because they speak this language. And visions of the future have the power to motivate us insofar as they speak this language. It's time we internalize our theology *in this language*!

To put it in terms of the first *Matrix* movie, if you're going to get free from the Matrix, you've got to wage war within the Matrix. Neo, Trinity, and Morpheus don't free humanity by theorizing about their bondage. They go back in and fight the agents within the virtual reality the agents themselves created. They play by the rules of the Matrix and learn how to bend the rules. In other words, you've got to battle concrete, experiential lies with concrete, experiential truths.

The Battle for Your Mind

Do you want to free your mind? Are you sufficiently angry that your brain—and thus your entire sense of reality—has been almost entirely *given to* you rather than *chosen by* you? Are you adequately disgusted with the idea that much of your internal and external life is controlled by neurochips someone or something else planted in you? Are you weary of the "splinter in your brain" and hungry for abundant life in Christ?

Then we've got to fight within the rules of the Matrix and bend them to our advantage. Which is simply to say, we've got to battle for our minds within the rules that govern the brain's operation. Our true ideas have got to become at least as vivid, as concrete, and as experiential as our false ones. The theology in our minds has got to become as impacting as the beer commercials. Our vision of God has to become as concrete and attractive as the most beautiful movie we've ever seen and the most moving symphony we've ever heard. Our thoughts about our identity in Christ need to be as embodied as Doreen's memory of being covered with insects.

We need to *embody* all our true information by imaginatively seeing it, hearing it, feeling it, smelling it, and tasting it. And we need to install it at every point where we locate renegade Matrix neurochips. The triggers that used to activate virtual-reality lies need to instead activate virtual-reality truth.

Are you ready to wage war *within the Matrix*?

Exercise 4

Learning to Adjust Your Inner World

It's time to begin to experience the power we have to alter our re-presentations and thereby alter the emotions associated with them. We want you to experience the shift in feeling that occurs when you purposely change aspects of your thought world. More specifically, we want you to experience the connection between the modality and submodality distinctions you employ in doing a particular memory, on the one hand, and the emotion you experience in doing this particular memory, on the other.

Our goal in this exercise isn't to permanently fix or alter anything. Like Neo in his first training session with Morpheus in the virtual-reality training room, we want you to discover your ability to alter your re-presentations and thus your emotions. We want you to begin to learn how to "bend the rules" of the Matrix. (In part 2 we'll learn how to permanently alter our inner virtual reality.)

We're going to ask you to individually recall the four memories you worked on in exercise 3 (that is, at different times recall a pleasant memory, a frustrated or angry memory, a fearful memory, and a sad memory). Follow the instructions below as you vividly recall each of these memories. Notice if altering the modality and submodality distinctions changes the emotional component of the memory.

Some may find that the emotion intensifies or diminishes when they alter their memories. Others may find that in some cases the emotion completely changes. Simply notice these things and write your observations in the space provided or in a journal. We again strongly encourage the reader to work through this exercise. Though it may be difficult for some at first, discovering how your mind works and the power you have over it is absolutely essential to setting your mind free to experience real life in Christ.

1. *If you see anything in your memory, make it bigger and note any changes in how the memory feels. Then make it smaller and note any changes in feeling.*

    Pleasant memory

    Angry memory

    Fearful memory

    Sad memory

2. *If your memory is in color, change it to black and white. If it is in black and white, change it to color. Note any changes in the emotional dimension of your memory.*

    Pleasant memory

    Angry memory

    Fearful memory

    Sad memory

3. *If the memory is a still frame (like a photograph or a snapshot) change it to a video (that is, give it motion). If it was like a video, make it a still frame. Note any change in the feeling of the memory.*

Pleasant memory

Angry memory

Fearful memory

Sad memory

4. *If you experience the memory from the perspective you originally had (associated)—that is, through your own eyes, ears, skin, etc.—step out of yourself and see yourself in the memory from a third-person perspective (disassociated). If you see yourself (your body) in your memory, step into yourself and experience it from the perspective you originally had (through your eyes). Note any ways this alters the emotion of the memory.*

Pleasant memory

Angry memory

Fearful memory

Sad memory

5. *If there is no sound in your memory, think of the event and notice if there was any sound at the time of the event; if so, then add it. Now gradually raise the volume until it's extremely loud. Then gradually lower the volume until it's completely off. Note any change in how the memory feels when you do this.*

Pleasant memory

Angry memory

Fearful memory

Sad memory

6. *If you have physical feeling as part of your memory (e.g., wind blowing against your face, warmth of the sun, rocks on your feet), delete it (that is, make yourself numb). If there is no physical feeling in your memory, add it. Note any change in how this affects the feeling of the memory.*

Pleasant memory

Angry memory

Fearful memory

Sad memory

7. *If smell is part of your memory, delete it. If smell isn't part of your memory, add it. Note any alterations in the emotional component of the memory.*

Pleasant memory

Angry memory

Fearful memory

Sad memory

8. *If taste is part of your memory, delete it. If taste wasn't part of your memory, add it. (If there was nothing to taste in the original event, imagine yourself eating a chocolate bar or drinking a Pepsi.) Notice if this alters the emotion of the memory.*

Pleasant memory

Angry memory

Fearful memory

Sad memory

If you did this exercise carefully, you undoubtedly found that while some modifications of the modality and submodality distinctions made little or no impact on the emotional component of your memory, others altered it significantly. The emotion either intensified or diminished, and in some cases perhaps changed altogether. When altering an aspect of the VAKOG code of a memory changes its emotional component, it means that that particular modality or submodality distinction is a *driver* of the emotion. For example, if your pleasant emotion involves hearing a beautiful symphony, deleting or even lowering the auditory component of the memory will undoubtedly alter the pleasantness of the memory. In this case *the meaning* of the memory (pleasantness) is *driven* by your internal auditory modality.

Our goal thus far has simply been to acquaint you with the fact that you do thought with a VAKOG code—re-presenting aspects of your experience on the inside—and that you have power to alter the meaning of a memory by altering this code. In the second part of this work we shall learn how to utilize this information to alter what we internally experience. We shall learn how to escape the Matrix and bring every thought captive to Christ.

PART 2
Escaping the Matrix

5

Opening Up Our Eyes

Getting Free from Matrix Images of God

MORPHEUS: The Matrix is everywhere. . . . It is the world that has been pulled over your eyes to blind you from the truth.

———∞———

When one turns to the Lord, the veil is removed. Now the Lord is the Spirit, and where the Spirit of the Lord is, there is freedom. And all of us, with unveiled faces, seeing the glory of the Lord as though reflected in a mirror, are being transformed into the same image from one degree of glory to another; for this comes from the Lord, the Spirit.

2 Corinthians 3:16–18 NRSV

Philip said, "Lord, show us the Father and that will be enough for us." Jesus answered: "Don't you know me, Philip, even after I have been among you such a long time? Anyone who has seen me has seen the Father. How can you say, 'Show us the Father'?"

John 14:8–9

We've learned what the Matrix is and how it works. It's now time to begin to learn how to escape it. It's time to begin to experience freedom. The place to begin is with the lie that is the foundation of the Matrix. It is a lie that affects almost all of us to one degree or another and strongly influences every other lie we experience as real. It is therefore the first and foremost lie we need to confront. It is the lie about who God is.

We're not talking about what we *consciously believe* about God. We're talking about how we *actually do* "belief in God" in our minds. We're talking about deceptive re-presentations that constitute our deep structure meaning of *God*. We're talking about Matrix neurochips about God.

The Foundational Lie

The first thing the serpent went after in the Garden of Eden story in Genesis 3 was Eve's view of God. "'You will not surely die,' the serpent said to the woman. 'For God knows that when you eat of it your eyes will be opened, and you will be like God, knowing good and evil'" (vv. 4–5). He influenced Eve to believe that God was not the all-loving, all-powerful, truthful God she had previously thought. The serpent made it seem as though God had duped Adam and Eve by telling them the forbidden tree would bring death. He made it seem that God didn't give them this "No Trespassing" sign out of love for their own good. Indeed, he made it appear that God's motivation in forbidding this tree was that he didn't want any competitors. So, the serpent suggested, if Adam and Eve were to have their eyes "opened," they needed to eat from the forbidden tree. In reality, it was the act of believing the serpent and eating from the tree that closed their eyes and blinded them to the truth.

This lie about God is directly or indirectly behind all lies. It is impossible to have a wrong view of God and have a consistently right view of anything else—the world, oneself, other people, the purpose of life, etc.—because the proper view of everything is related to its relationship to the true God.

It is no surprise, therefore, that when Adam and Eve accepted a lie about God, they instantly found themselves immersed in a lie about themselves. Whereas they were created to experience fullness of life out of their relationship with God, they now experienced themselves as empty, attempting to fill their emptiness with the forbidden wisdom of the tree. Whereas they were created to receive life from God for free, they now experienced themselves as people who needed to *do* something (eat from the tree) to try to attain fullness of life. Whereas God created them to live in total openness and honesty before him and one another, they now experienced themselves as people who needed to hide from each other and from God.[1]

All of our emotions toward God are associated with our mental images of him. What impacts our disposition toward God most is not our conscious beliefs about God—the Matrix is never primarily about conceptual information—but our actual re-presentations of God. To the extent that our re-presentations are skewed, our emotional response to God will be skewed and our lives will correspondingly suffer. At the foundation of the Matrix are deceptive re-presentations of God.

Jill's Theological Neurochip

Jill was a student in one of my (Greg's) theology classes. Her theology was solid. She knew the creeds and confessions of the church well. She had the right list of God's omni-attributes (omniscient, omnipotent, omnipresent), the right list of verses proving the deity of Christ, the orthodox perspective on pneumatology, soteriology, ecclesiology, angelology, eschatology, and every other religious "ology." She was exceptionally intelligent, well versed in the Bible, and relatively mature in her faith.

Yet Jill had no passion. None. Indeed, Jill felt no emotional connection with God or with anything having to do with Christianity. Related to this (though Jill wasn't yet aware of this connection), she had struggled for years with a preoccupation with her looks and with an eating disorder that went along with it.

Jill shared all this with me one day after class. She wondered what was wrong with her. Why was it that some of her friends seemed to get excited about God, seemed to have a passion for doing his work, and seemed to even get emotional once in a while during worship services while she felt "as flat as a doornail"? She dutifully did all the things Christians "are supposed to do"—go to church, read the Bible, pray, etc. But she felt as though she was "just going through the motions." She wondered out loud if God had perhaps given up on her because of her carnal preoccupation with her looks and with her eating issues.

I quickly reassured Jill that God would never give up on her for *any* reason. If Jesus loved her so much he was willing to go to Calvary to spend eternity with her, he wasn't about to abandon her because her brain was a bit messed up about the importance of her looks. I suggested to her that, if anything, the opposite might be the case. That is, I strongly suspected that her feeling of abandonment was contributing to her preoccupation with her looks and her eating issues rather than the other way around.

Knowing that all our emotions are associated with the concrete visual, auditory, and kinesthetic images we have in our heads, I asked Jill what her picture of God was. She was puzzled by the question, for she had already proven herself an outstanding student in my class. But with my coaxing, she finally gave me the "officially correct answer." She told me that God is omniscient, omnipotent, omnipresent, etc.

That was *not* what I was looking for. "What is your *real* picture of God?" I asked. "Forget your theology for a moment. When you think of God, what comes to your mind? What do you see or hear? Examine your thoughts," I continued. "Do you see, hear, or feel anything in your mind when you think about God?"

It took a little while for Jill to even realize that she had concrete pictures, words, and sensations in her mind associated with the word *God*. This is not atypical. Most of us are largely unaware of the virtual reality inside our heads, and some of us are totally oblivious to it. When Jill finally began to get in touch with how she did her re-presentation of God, she was shocked. The conversation that followed went like this:

> **GREG:** Try to calmly observe what goes on in your head when you think of God. Is there anything you see, hear, or feel when you think of God? Say to yourself, "Soul, listen up. Tell me what you really believe about God."
>
> **JILL:** [*closes her eyes and pauses for a few moments*] He's not interested.
>
> **GREG:** *God's* not interested?

JILL: Right.

GREG: How do you know this, Jill? Do you see something or hear something when you think of God? Watch and listen to what happens in your inner world when you think of God.

JILL: I hear a voice.

GREG: Tell me exactly what you hear.

JILL: It says to me, "He's not interested in you."

GREG: Good. Is it your voice or someone else's voice?

JILL: It's my own voice.

GREG: Interesting. Now, are you seeing anything in your mind?

JILL: [*again closes her eyes for a brief moment*] Yeah, I do! Weird. I'm seeing a large canyon, like the Grand Canyon.

GREG: Describe it for me in as much detail as you can.

JILL: I don't know. It's huge. Kind of majestic. All rocky, barren, dry.

GREG: Is your picture in color?

JILL: This is *so* weird! Yes. The sky is blue and the dirt is brown.

GREG: Is there motion in the picture or is it a still frame?

JILL: [*laughs a little*] It seems there's wind. My hair is blowing.

GREG: Do you see yourself in the picture?

JILL: No. I don't see myself.

GREG: Then how do you know your hair is blowing?

JILL: I guess I feel it.

GREG: Great. So you're experiencing the canyon through your own eyes?

JILL: [*laughing, nodding yes*] This is bizarre!

GREG: Do you see anything else?

JILL: [*again takes a moment to discover what she's seeing*] I'm at the edge of one side of the canyon, and I see another person on the other side.

GREG: Who do you think it is?

JILL: Well, I can't really see him. He's way on the other side. He's facing away from me. But I know it's Jesus.

GREG: How do you know?

JILL: I just do.

GREG: Okay. You're looking at Jesus on the other side of the canyon facing away from you. Tell me if you see, hear, or feel anything else. [*Jill pauses for a moment, and then, quite suddenly, her countenance changes. While she had been rather lighthearted, even giddy, with a tinge of awkwardness up to this point, she now becomes visibly stressed and saddened.*]

GREG: Tell me what's going on, Jill.

JILL: I feel so lonely. Why won't he turn and face me? I feel like I want to call to him, "I'm over here." But he's not interested.

GREG: How do you know that?

JILL: It's like there's another camera giving a close-up of his face. I can see him at a distance across the canyon but also this shot up close.

GREG: Is there any motion or sound in the close-up shot?

JILL: He hears my voice from a distance, like an echo in the canyon. But he just looks out into the distance. He even seems annoyed by my calling to him. His hair is blowing. There's motion.

GREG: Good job.

It's not surprising that Jill felt no passion for God, is it? Anyone who re-presented God the way Jill did would find it impossible to feel passionate about him. As often happens, although Jill had a lot of correct conceptual information about God, her *actual mental re-presentation* was far from truth. And it was her actual re-presentation, not her information, with which her emotions were associated and thus had implications for her life.

We could spend a great deal of time trying to figure out exactly how Jill acquired this deceptive picture of God. It likely had something to do with the fact that she was the second to the youngest child in a very large family and often felt ignored. It might also have had something to do with the fact that her family (especially her father) was emotionally quite stoic. But

I didn't know any of this at the time of this conversation, and it really didn't matter.

Finding out how a person got a neurochip installed is not as important as learning how the neurochip misre-presents reality *in the present*. The important question is not, *"Why* are you the way you are?" but rather, "How do *you do* the way you are?" Not only this, but answering the *why* question often takes a great deal of time, effort, and speculation, as well as money (if done in professional therapy). And even when you think you've found the right answer, this doesn't help debug the neurochip. It just tells you who or what to blame for it being there! It gives you information but doesn't itself transform you.

The question that empowers you to change is, "How do you *do* [in your mind] the way you are?" It's your organic computer, and you have the authority to program it. In Jill's case, the question was, "How do you *do* 'being emotionally distant from God'?" And the answer was in part found in her deep structure re-presentation of God with which her emotional state was associated. This was something she could—and did—do something about, and it didn't take years of therapy to do it.

The True Picture of God

I reminded Jill of the most foundational truth in all of Christianity: God is fully revealed in the person of Jesus Christ. You see, Jill's experience of a distant, uninterested God was *real* to her, but it was not *true*. This is the essence of the Matrix: we experience as real things that are not true. All mental and spiritual sickness is the result of the gap between what we experience as real and what is in fact true. To move toward wholeness, we have to close the gap. We have to "take captive every thought to make it obedient to Christ" (2 Cor. 10:5). We have to cease experiencing lies and start experiencing truth.

Jill needed to learn how to collapse her deceptive re-presentation of God and learn how to see and experience the true God revealed in Jesus Christ. Jesus said he is "the truth" (John 14:6). The Greek word for truth (*aleithia*) literally means "uncovered." Jesus is the truth about God because in him the deception the serpent used to blind us to the true God is removed. Jesus uncovers the true God!

This is why Jesus is called the Word of God: his very being communicates who God is (John 1:1). So too, the Bible says that no one can see God in his infinite essence, but Jesus, the Son of God, has made him known (John 1:18). He is called "the image of God" because in him the infinite God is incarnate and revealed (2 Cor. 4:4; Col. 1:15). For this reason the Bible says, "The Son is the radiance of God's glory and the exact representation of his being" (Heb. 1:3). In fact, when Philip asked Jesus to show him God the Father, Jesus said, "Don't you know *me*, Philip . . . ? Anyone who has seen *me* has seen *the Father*. How can you say, 'Show us the Father'?" (John 14:9, emphasis added). It is no wonder, then, that believers are encouraged to fix their spiritual eyes on Jesus (Heb. 12:2; see also Col. 3:1–5).

Indeed, according to Paul, we are transformed as we behold the radiance of God's glory in the face of Jesus Christ. And Paul makes it clear that this seeing takes place *in our minds*. "The god of this age has blinded *the minds* of unbelievers," Paul writes, "so that they cannot *see* the light of the gospel of the glory of Christ, who is the image of God" (2 Cor. 4:4, emphasis added). Our *minds* or hearts have been made "dull" and a "veil" has been placed over them (2 Cor. 3:14–15). But when we turn to Christ, Paul says, the veil in our minds is "taken away" (2 Cor. 3:16). We are now able "with unveiled faces" to see "the glory of the Lord as though reflected in a mirror" and are consequently "transformed into the same image from one degree of glory to another" (2 Cor. 3:18 NRSV). For all who submit to his lordship, God causes "his light [to] shine in our hearts to give us the light of the knowledge of the glory of God in the face of Christ" (2 Cor. 4:6).[2]

Paul is teaching us that we are transformed by what we experience in our minds! And the single most important thing to experience as vividly, as profoundly, and with as many senses as possible is Jesus Christ. As I informed Jill, our re-presentations about God—and therefore our emotional responses to God—will be as healthy as they are Christlike and as sick as they are non-Christlike. To take every thought about God captive to Christ, therefore, means to transform every God re-presentation into a Christlike re-presentation.

Jill's Experience of Truth

Knowing the truth about God is very important. But as a matter of fact, *Jill already knew this*, at least on a conceptual level. We'd covered it before in class. What Jill hadn't done was *experience* it; hence she wasn't transformed by it. While the lie of her re-presentation of God was concrete, the truth of the information she believed was abstract. Jill needed to take the lie captive to Christ and set her mind free to experience truth.

The Lord used the conversation that follows to lead Jill into an experience of truth.

GREG: Jill, I'd like you to go back to your Grand Canyon scene, just as you experienced it before. Got it?

JILL: I'm there.

GREG: Where's Jesus?

JILL: On the other side of the canyon, facing away from me, just like before.

GREG: Now you know that this scene is lying, don't you?

JILL: What do you mean?

GREG: Well, you know that Jesus died for you, right? You know he said he'd never leave you or forsake you. You know he dwells within all who accept him, and you accept him, right?

JILL: Yes.

GREG: So you know Jesus isn't far from you and doesn't face away from you. He's passionately in love with you, Jill. He's embracing you right now.

JILL: I know that, I guess. But it doesn't feel true.

GREG: Of course you don't *feel* Christ close to you and in love with you. You're re-presenting him as disinterested and on the other side of the Grand Canyon! Who'd feel close to a person like *that*? And of course this scene *feels* true, because it's the image you've always identified as real. But you know on the authority of God's Word that it's a lie!

JILL: Okay, it's a lie. It just doesn't feel like it.

GREG: The feelings will change as you align your thoughts with truth. Help me understand this feeling you are having. What would you label it?

We should at this point note that people always *feel* that their internal re-presentations of reality are true. If we make our present feelings the arbiter of truth, we will remain locked in our present re-presentations of which the feelings are part. Initially, our new re-presentations may feel unreal—like we are pretending. We'll see this happen with Jill. But if we make our new re-presentations vivid and concrete, before long the brain will identify the new re-presentation as real, and it will begin to feel true to us.

JILL: I feel shame.

GREG: Jill, say to that part of you that is feeling shame, "I know that you are feeling ashamed. But I will be able to help you in a few minutes."

JILL: [*pauses briefly*] That feels better, kind of like I am in charge.

GREG: Wonderful. Now let's change this scene so that you are able to re-present the truth that you already know about God in your life.

JILL: Change it?

GREG: Of course. It's *your* brain, Jill. They're *your* images. Some event or experience installed this meaning of your relationship with Jesus. It's your job to assess how this part is re-presenting your relationship with God. You are commanded and empowered to take all thoughts captive to the true Jesus. You know who the true Jesus is. But he's certainly not the one you're seeing in your head right now.

JILL: Okay. How do you change it?

GREG: Let's first pray. As we do, just keep your re-presentation in mind. The Bible tells us that the Holy Spirit's job is to point us to Jesus. This is why he's called "the Spirit of Truth" [John 16:13–14; see also 2 Cor. 3:16–18]. He uncovers the true

Jesus for us. He pulls back the lies in our minds that keep us from seeing the true God.

I then asked the Holy Spirit to help Jill remove lies in her mind and to empower her to see the true Jesus.

Greg: Okay, Jill, you know Jesus loves you and is interested in you, right?

Jill: Yes, but . . .

Greg: Remember, we will deal with the part of you that feels differently in a few minutes. Right now, concentrate on the truth. On the authority of God's Word, do you believe Jesus loves you?

Jill: Yes.

Greg: Good. Now, working with the Holy Spirit, we're going to have your brain accurately reflect what you believe to be true rather than a lie. The true Jesus wouldn't be facing away from you, would he?

Jill: I suppose not.

Greg: The true Jesus is not only facing you, he's running toward you, like the father of the prodigal son [Luke 15:11–32]. He's desperately searching for you, like the shepherd looking for the one lost sheep and the woman who lost her precious coin [Luke 15:3–10]. So in your mind allow Jesus to turn around and face you on the other side of the canyon.

Jill: [*pauses for a moment*] He won't turn!

Greg: It's *your* brain; it will do whatever you ask it to do.

Jill: You just want me to pretend that he's facing me?

Greg: Jesus *is* facing you! The fact that you feel you're pretending when you re-present this just shows how thoroughly you were deceived into mistaking a lying picture for a true one. I don't know when and how your false re-presentation of Jesus was installed, but what matters most right now is that you are an adult, you know the truth about Jesus, and you can work with the Holy Spirit to change your mind to re-

present this truth. With God's help, you can take thoughts
captive to make them obedient to Christ. So Jill, ask the Holy
Spirit to show you the truth about Jesus's love and grace.

JILL: [*tightens her eyes for a moment as she prays*] Okay, I think I
got it. I see Jesus facing me.

GREG: Wonderful. Describe for me what you see.

JILL: Well, he's still really far away. I can't make out his face.

GREG: Okay. Now the Bible tells you the real Jesus considered it joy
to die for you because he wants to spend eternity with you
[Heb. 12:2], right? The Bible says God pursues you when
you're lost, right? And the Bible says Jesus loves you with an
everlasting love [Jer. 31:3], right?

JILL: Yes.

GREG: Knowing this, what do you think the true Jesus would be
doing right now in your scene?

JILL: [*She pauses for a moment, and her voice cracks when she
finally speaks.*] He's waving to me. He notices *me*.

GREG: Holy Spirit, make the true Jesus come alive for Jill.

JILL: It seems like he's trying to get *my* attention. He's jumping up
and down and waving both arms.

At this point, Jill began to laugh and sob at the same time. All
of our emotions are associated with our mental re-presentations,
and Jill was finally beginning to have a re-presentation that
evoked positive emotions.

GREG: Of course he is! But I wonder if he's also waving his arms to
close the canyon—kind of like the reverse of what Moses did
when he parted the Red Sea.

JILL: What?

GREG: What's *true*, Jill? Is there *really* a canyon between you and
Jesus?

JILL: No.

GREG: That is the way a wounded little girl interpreted an experience a long time ago. And Jesus is healing that right now. Let Jesus close the canyon and come close to you.

JILL: It's a *huge* canyon!

GREG: To *you*, maybe, but not to *Jesus. He's* God, and it's *your* brain, Jill. So together I know you can close that stupid lie! Holy Spirit, help Jill close the canyon.

JILL: I don't know.

GREG: It's like an earthquake in reverse. Can you hear and feel the ground rumbling as the two sides come closer and closer together? You know the Holy Spirit is bringing you closer to truth. Just let him do it. [*As I pray, Jill pauses with her eyes intensely shut.*]

GREG: Talk to me, Jill. What's going on?

JILL: Jesus's side of the canyon was coming pretty close. But then it just stopped.

GREG: Why did you stop it?

JILL: I didn't. It just stopped.

GREG: It's your brain, Jill. You can make it do whatever you want, and you want truth. Close that gulf till there isn't even a crack left!

JILL: I'm scared. The closer Jesus's side of the canyon gets to me, the more scared I get.

GREG: That's good, Jill. Now we know why you stopped it. What are you afraid of?

JILL: Him! I've been such a disappointment! I'm so ashamed of the way I've been so preoccupied with my appearance and purging and stuff.

While Jill's sense of emotional distance was due to her image of Jesus being distant and disinterested, we at this point were uncovering an even deeper motivation for why she continued to image Jesus in this fashion. It was, as it often is, shame. Shame is rooted in a lie that our worth before God is based on what we do rather than on what he did on Calvary.

In an ideal counseling situation, I would have explored the possibility that Jill's shame was associated to *other* neurochips. This may have led to inner child work such as we shall illustrate in chapter 8. In the educational context in which I operated with Jill, however, I knew this meeting was likely the only chance I'd have to help Jill at this level. Hence I continued my focus on Jill's current re-presentation of God.

GREG: Jill, Jesus didn't die for you because you were perfect. He died for you and for me because *we're not!* And it's only when we accept that we're loved in the midst of our imperfections that we give him a chance to grow us out of our imperfections. Jill, Jesus loves you exactly as you are, despite your shortcomings. Let him come close to you.

JILL: I just don't know if I can face him.

GREG: How far away is he right now?

JILL: Not far. I can almost see his face.

GREG: Good. I want you to see Jesus cup his hands over his mouth and say—or shout if he needs to—things he's already told you are true in his Word.

JILL: Like what?

GREG: Hear Jesus say, "Jill, I will never hurt you or shame you. I told you I will never leave you nor forsake you. Never! I love you with an everlasting and perfect love." Can you hear Jesus say this?

JILL: Yes.

GREG: Hear him say, "I've made you ravishingly beautiful, Jill, just as you are, whether you or anyone else can see that or not. I died for you just because I want to be close to you. You're my bride, Jill. I'm your groom. Your sin is no match for my endless love and grace. We're going to heal your wounds, you'll see. But I already know your heart, Jill, and your sin is already forgiven. I want to look into your eyes. I want to embrace you in my love. Let me close this space between us, Jill." Hear Jesus say, "Don't be afraid. The burning love I

showed you on Calvary is the same burning love I have for
you right now."

After a moment, Jill began to cry. She did so for a long while.
I could see the canyon had been closed. For the first time in as
long as Jill could remember, she *felt* something positive toward
Jesus. And it was beautiful.

Anyone who experienced in their minds what Jill had been
experiencing up to this point would have felt apathy, if not animosity, toward God. But by the same means, anyone whose
innermost being is surrendered to God and who experiences
the true Jesus in his or her mind cannot help but be moved and
drawn toward him. He *is* a beautiful God!

This was the beginning of a transformation in Jill's relationship with God. Jill began to regularly experience love, joy, and
passion in her walk with God.

As is often the case, the renegade neurochip I helped debug
from Jill's brain was actually a part of a system of renegade
neurochips. Neural-nets are networked with other neural-nets.
In other words, Jill's re-presentation of Jesus on the far side of a
canyon was just one of a number of deceptive re-presentations
she had about God and herself. In other contexts—with different triggers—Jill heard, saw, and felt other images of a distant,
disinterested God. Collapsing this one deceptive re-presentation
weakened, but did not destroy, the entire network.

Consequently, Jill had to learn how to become a constant
detective of her brain. She learned that whenever she was experiencing apathy or abandonment in relation to God, it was
associated with something she herself was doing in her mind.
She learned to trace these feelings back to the re-presentations
with which they were associated. She learned how to examine her
thoughts in accordance with the way she actually did them—as
words, pictures, and sensations. Knowing the truth, and with the
help of some subsequent counseling, Jill gradually learned how
to take each of them captive to make it obedient to Christ.

With each victory, the overall network was weakened. And a
daughter of the king was being set free from the Matrix.

The Healing of Jill's Appearance Orientation

We should end by noting how this inner transformation affected Jill's struggle with a preoccupation with looks and her eating disorder. It wasn't long after my encounter with Jill that she began to change her strategy for fulfillment.

All of our attitude and behavioral struggles are in one way or another futile attempts on our part to fill an inner vacuum. We were created to receive and experience abundant life from God, which includes experiencing unconditional and unsurpassable worth, and to reflect this life to others out of the fullness of our hearts. When we, like Adam and Eve, embrace a deep structure lie about God, it disrupts the flow of God's abundant life into us and through us. We consequently try to acquire life from the only other thing we know is real—our world. So we try to establish our worth on the basis of what we can do, who we can impress, what we can acquire, etc. We're trying desperately to earn through our effort what God has always wanted to give us for free. This is life lived under a lie; this is life in the Matrix.

There are about as many different carnal strategies for getting life as there are individual people in the world. Jill's strategy was associated with her appearance, especially her physical shape. In a culture in which young people—especially women—are constantly bombarded with graphic images that in various ways communicate a message that life is to be found in being skinny, beautiful, sexy, etc., this is hardly surprising. One out of four teenage girls in America share Jill's struggle at some point.

One could focus on Jill's behavior, shame her for her preoccupation with looks, provide her with accurate theological and biological information, etc. But as long as the actual words, pictures, and sensations in Jill's head remained the same, she would experience an irresistible urge to look stunning and avoid eating or purge herself when she binged. As we have said, *whoever controls the neural-nets controls the life*. The neurochips that suppressed the truth about God and thus the truth about Jill's worth had to be altered if her behavior was ever to change.

As Jill brought her actual re-presentations of God into alignment with the true God, revealed in Jesus Christ, she began to experience the real life that is found in Christ. The neurological blockages that formerly prevented this abundant life from flowing into her and out of her were being torn down. The more she experienced real life, the less she needed to seek after the shallow, surrogate, unsatisfying life of impressing people with her looks and body shape.

This isn't to suggest that Jill had no more struggles in this area. On the contrary, she had major strongholds, derived from millions of commercials and other influences, which communicated lies to her about what she actually looked like and how important her looks were. Under the right circumstances, these would continue to be triggered.

But the more Jill experienced real life in Christ, the weaker these triggered neurochips became. Not only this, but the more she learned how to effectively be a detective of her brain, the better she got at quickly locating a lie when she felt it and uninstalling it. Whenever Jill felt empty or fat or insecure about herself, she traced these emotions back to the re-presentations in her mind with which they were associated and brought them into alignment with truth.

Jill learned how to be a "detective of her brain." She was on her way out of the Matrix, into freedom, into experiencing *real* life in Christ.

Exercise 5

Experiencing Jesus

The goal of this exercise is to help you experience the true God, revealed in Jesus Christ, as real. It is based on a traditional form of spirituality that involves praying with (not *to*) mental and physical images. This tradition, called "cataphatic spirituality," understands that thought is as impacting and transforming as it is concrete, vivid, and experiential. It is most fundamentally rooted in Paul's teaching that we are transformed by mentally beholding the glory of God in the face of Jesus Christ (2 Cor. 3:16–4:6).[3] This exercise is broken down into five steps.

Step 1: Block out a half hour or more when you can be alone. Dim the lights and put on some soft, beautiful background music. Music is a gift that affects us all in varying degrees, and it can be used in service to God when it helps us open our hearts to the Lord and become more pliable in his gentle hands. We recommend that the music be without lyrics because words will likely distract you.

Step 2: Spend some time in prayer asking the Holy Spirit to point you to Jesus in as vivid and real a way as possible (John 16:13–14). Ask him to remove any veil over your mind that blinds you to truth and to set you free to experience the glory of God in the face of Jesus Christ (2 Cor. 3:17–4:6).

Step 3: Re-present a place in your mind that evokes a pleasant and peaceful feeling. It may be a place in your past, associated with a pleasant experience, or it may be simply a place you imagine on your own. Notice what you see, hear, and/or sense that makes this place pleasant. Adjust the submodality distinctions to intensify the pleasantness of this place. Notice what you see, hear, sense, smell, and perhaps taste in this scene.

Step 4: Re-present Jesus meeting you in this place as vividly as you are re-presenting the place itself. As you do so, remind yourself that he is the one who loves you so much he died for you. Remind yourself that all you can and need to know about God is found in Jesus. If you are able, see his perfect love for you in his eyes, for eyes are the windows of the soul. Then re-present him coming over to you and embracing you.

Step 5: See, hear, and feel Jesus personally communicate to you things God has already said about you in Scripture. You already know these things are true, for they are in his Word. But now you are going to experience them personalized toward *you*. He begins each sentence with your name. See and hear Jesus say in a soft, caring voice:

- "[Your name], I love you more than you could possibly imagine. I could not love you more than I do right now. I love you with an everlasting love. You are my beloved child and my radiant bride."
- "[Your name], I sing and dance over you! I rejoice that I've found you and you're mine. I will never leave you nor forsake you—never! I considered it a joy to give my life so we can be together eternally."
- "[Your name], I know you better than you know yourself—and I love you. I know your struggles and your wounds,

and together we're going to conquer the struggles and heal the wounds. You're going to shine like the sun when we're through."

There may be parts of you that resist experiencing Jesus in this intimate way. For example, some may hear an internal voice say, "You're making this up," or, "You know this can't be true." Others may feel a sense of shame. In subsequent chapters we'll talk about how to bring these parts into alignment with truth. For right now, simply say to yourself, "On God's authority, I receive this as true," and allow Jesus to speak to you again and embrace you. By allowing Jesus to love you in the midst of your Matrix thoughts, you are permitting him to love you out of your Matrix thoughts.

We recommend that you regularly encounter the living Jesus in this fashion. All genuine growth in our lives, and all healthy spiritual activity, is the result of our resting in an experience of the true God loving us for free—not because of what we do, but just because of who we are and who he is.

6

Taking the Red Pill

Experiencing the True You

MEROVINGIAN: You see there is only one constant, one universal; it is the only real truth. Causality, action, reaction, cause, and effect. . . . Choice is an illusion created between those with power and those without. . . . Causality, there is no escape from it; we are forever slaves to it.

———∞∞∞———

Then you will know the truth, and the truth will set you free. . . . I tell you the truth, everyone who sins is a slave to sin. . . . If the Son sets you free, you will be free indeed.

John 8:32, 34, 36

What Is *Real* and What Is *True*

If you are like most believers, the *you* that you experience is not the *real you*. The *real you* is trapped inside the *you* that is conformed to the Matrix of the world. "A world has been pulled over your eyes," as Morpheus told Neo. The *you* that you experience is the *you* that has been largely defined by your upbringing, your past experiences, the culture into which you're submerged, the media that bombards you, and the false conclusions at which you've arrived by the distorted operations of your own fallen brain. To the extent that this *you* doesn't agree with the *you* that is in Christ Jesus, the *you* you experience is a lie.

The *you* that you experience as real is the total constellation of neural-net installations in your brain. It is the Matrix *you* if these neural-net installations do not accord with truth. If the *you* that you experience is not the *true you*, you have been defined from the bottom up rather than the top down, and the outside in rather than the inside out (see chapter 4). Insofar as our experience of ourselves is out of sync with what God says about us, our experience of ourselves is deceptive. We are, to this degree, robotic extensions of others' designs and slaves within the Matrix.

The problem is that we empower the Matrix to define us when we accept that what we experience as *real* is also *true*. If we assume that our map (experience) is the territory (truth), we can't hope to adjust our map to bring it into alignment with the true territory. When sincere believers say things such as, "I am worthless," "I'm hopeless," "God doesn't care about me," or, "That's just the way I am," we can know this reflects what feels *real* to them. But if we believe the Bible (our reliable guide to the true territory), these sentiments certainly do not reflect *truth*.

It's important to remember that our organic computers are hardwired to draw conclusions about "what is real" on the basis of our experiences. This hardwiring works well when experience installs true beliefs because then our beliefs about what is real match what is true. But it works against us insofar as experience installs lies. For then our sense of *real* is out of sync with truth—but we will not know it until something calls into question our sense of what is real. We are trapped in our false experience of what is real. We are trapped in the Matrix.

For Neo to escape the Matrix, he had to first doubt his life-long feeling that the Matrix was true reality. All freedom from deception begins with doubt.

To illustrate, I (Al) missed a great deal of school when I was growing up, chiefly because my family was extremely dysfunctional. I spent many days as a youngster skipping school and playing in bars while my father drank. Consequently, from the start I was always behind other students. I honestly didn't know the whole alphabet until I was in my early teens! My delayed learning, combined with persistent teasing from peers and ridiculing from adults, convinced me that I was stupid. Not only this, but in the environment in which I grew up, asking questions wasn't seen as evidence of intelligent inquisitiveness but as further evidence of one's ignorance. I thus developed a phobia about learning that ensured I would remain behind other students, which intensified my conviction that I was stupid.

My feeling that I was stupid was very *real* to me through my teen years. But I now know it wasn't *true*. When I was eventually able to get into an environment in which asking questions was rewarded rather than punished, I discovered that I'm able to learn quickly. Counter-examples of academic success allowed me to doubt my stupidity and eventually empowered me to form a new belief: I am, as a matter of fact, intellectually competent.

This is how it works for each of us. To bring any belief into alignment with truth, we must first doubt our belief, even though it *feels* real. We have to question our *map* (experience) if we are going to adjust it to the true *territory* (truth). It's absolutely vital that we vigilantly preserve this distinction between what *feels real* to us and what is in fact *true*. To the extent that we don't do this, we will remain locked in our present deceptive experience of what feels real. We will, in other words, remain trapped in the Matrix.

In fact, when we automatically assume that what we experience as real is true, we are surrendering our ability and responsibility to take control of our thoughts and bring them into alignment with truth as defined by God. We are basically agreeing with the Merovingian, the French ruler who appears in *The Matrix Reloaded* (the second *Matrix* movie) and who espouses the belief that "we are forever slaves" to causality. We are empowering every deceptive message we've ever internalized to define us the rest of our lives, making ourselves slaves of our neurochips and thereby slaves to whomever or whatever installed them, "for people are slaves to whatever masters them" (2 Peter

2:19 NRSV). Tragically, we are reduced to being the mere effect of causes set in motion years earlier or causes impacting us in the present.

The little brother with a jar of bugs, the frustrated father building a swing set, Al's dad, Greg's grandmother, or the momentary news flash of a crashing airplane become the causal lords of a portion of our lives. For whoever or whatever controls the neurons controls the life. And whoever or whatever controls the life is to that degree "lord" of the life.

If we are to free our minds to experience real life under the lordship of Jesus Christ, we must resolve that *our feelings, however real, are not a credible source for what is* true.

The central question of the first and second movies of the *Matrix* trilogy is, "Are humans free, or are we governed by fate and by outside forces?" Is the Merovingian—and the Architect, and (interestingly enough) Morpheus—right in believing everything happens according to a predesigned blueprint? Or is Neo right in believing humans can, with effort, transcend the vicious cycle of cause and effect?

God Created You to Be Free!

Neo is decisively on the side of the Bible. As much as we are influenced by factors outside ourselves, *humans are free*, and as a result we are responsible for our thoughts and behaviors. True, our self-chosen sin enslaves us to the point that we cannot on our own choose God without the Holy Spirit's help (1 Cor. 12:3). But even those who remain enslaved to sin retain some power over their thoughts, attitudes, and behaviors. In any case, God is at work in the world through his Holy Spirit to enable everybody to choose God if they will yield to him.

Yet, from a biblical perspective, our freedom to choose is not our highest freedom. Indeed, it is but a provisional form of freedom. *Ultimate* freedom is the freedom to experience life as God intended it. *Ultimate* freedom is the freedom that comes from experiencing truth (John 8:32). *Ultimate* freedom is the freedom to participate in God's love and to thus live life out of fullness rather than out of emptiness. But to experience this ultimate freedom, we must use our provisional freedom to choose it. We must choose to align our thoughts with God's truth. We must choose to exercise our power to adjust our internal maps (experience) to accurately reflect the territory (truth) as defined by God. We must choose to have no other lord than Jesus Christ. We must choose to be defined from the top down and inside out. In other words, we must freely choose to be ultimately free.

Of course, if you are a follower of Jesus you have already made him Lord of your life—at least in principle. This surrender in your innermost being gives you your new identity. But choosing to allow Christ to be Lord over your life *in principle* is one thing; doing so in *actual life* is quite another. To experience the freedom and life of Jesus Christ, we must choose to have him be Lord over our thoughts on a moment-by-moment basis. We must vigilantly take *every* thought captive to Christ (2 Cor. 10:5). To the extent that we don't do this, our new identity will remain an abstract truth devoid of experiential content. We will experience ourselves in actual life as being other than we truly are in Christ.

Indeed, to the extent that we do not choose to align our internal re-presentations with the truth that is in Christ, our thoughts are chosen for us. We allow ourselves to be defined by experiences of the past rather than by our Creator. We are defined from the bottom up and the outside in rather than the top down and inside out. We enthrone as functional lord our alcoholic father, our frustrated grandmother, our mischievous little brother, or any other person or event that installed lies in our lives.

To the extent that we do not take authority over our thoughts, someone or something else does. We allow ourselves to be slaves to causality. We vote *yes* to the Merovingian's fatalism.

We can't begin to make headway in experiencing the abundant life we've been given in Christ until we firmly vote *no* to the Merovingian's fatalism. On the authority of God's Word, we must choose to believe we *can* change. Just because we've always been a certain way doesn't mean we have to continue to be that way. True, much of how we experience ourselves *right now* may not have been chosen by us, and we may have thus far been largely shaped by our past experiences. *But this doesn't mean that we have to remain this way.*

Believe in the possibility of change. Take the red pill! You are a slave to no one except Christ, the Lord of love.

■ ■

Freedom from a Painful Past

What grounds our confidence in the possibility of change is the unsurpassable love of God. God never gives up on us! If anyone seemed beyond hope of change, it was me (Al). By the age of nine, the Matrix had thoroughly infiltrated my mind. From as early as I can remember, I was physically, sexually, and emotionally abused. Most of it came from people who were supposed to love me and often by people who (usually in drunken stupors) said they loved me. My young mind quickly came to the Matrix-inspired conclusion that the meaning of *love* was pain. My deep structure meaning of *love* was "vulnerability to abuse." My VAKOG code for *love* was something too ugly and too graphic to print here.

As a result, throughout my childhood and into my early adult years I felt nothing but fear when anyone said or otherwise indicated that they loved me. Believing Matrix lies about myself and others, I was empty, because like everyone else I was made to be filled with unconditional love. And the flesh-strategy I adopted to fill this void was to make myself as invincible as possible. Consequently, I trusted no one. I learned to rely completely on myself.

As is always the case, my Matrix beliefs hindered my capacity to hear the Good News of Jesus Christ. In fact, when I first heard the message of God's love, I felt scared. It meant that if I accepted this "love," God would abuse me. When people pointed to the crucified Christ as evidence of this love, it only served to confirm my Matrix deep structure meaning of *love*: the God of love abuses his own Son! Clearly, the "god of this age" had thoroughly "blinded" my eyes so I could not "see the light of the gospel of the glory of Christ, who is the image of God" (2 Cor. 4:4). I was thoroughly trapped in the Matrix. No one who knew me back then thought there was any hope for me.

But *God* held out hope. Because of his incomprehensible love, God relentlessly pursued me. God continually brought into my life strong counter-examples to my demented Matrix beliefs about love. Chief among these were my wife and son. Through the patient love of my wife and the unconditional love of my son, a love that never harmed me, I slowly began to doubt what I previously assumed was *real*. Over years I cautiously let my wife and son into my life. I slowly learned the beauty of being vulnerable to others. Little by little I learned to trust. Inch by inch I learned the true meaning of love. My deep structure meaning of *love* as "pain" was slowly transformed. As my neurochip beliefs about love were transformed, so was the gospel message. In time, I could actually hear it as the Good News it truly is, and I surrendered my life to Christ. As I learned of my true identity in Christ, I gradually learned how to take captive all my previous Matrix re-presentations about love. I developed entirely new filters through the Word and the Spirit that allowed me to increasingly experience truth. While I still discover triggers that activate old Matrix neurochips about love, about my intellectual competence, and about a multitude of other things, everyone who knew the old Al Larson is amazed at how completely God has transformed me.

Though the abuse in my past was severe, and though the first three decades of my life were spent living on autopilot as a slave to this pain-filled past, this did not have to determine *how I would continue to be*. I was not doomed to live a loveless life!

As children we did not have the cognitive resources to distinguish between what is real and what is true. But as free, thinking, and responsible adults, we can know the truth, and the truth can set us free! As children we could not escape the evil intentions of the Matrix world. But as believing adults we have access to a power that transcends any evil. As children we could be threatened, manipulated, and coerced. But as adults we can trust that we've been given a spirit of fearlessness, power, and self-control (2 Tim. 1:7). As children we may have been victimized by unfortunate circumstances or evil intentions, but we are not children any longer. We can trust that in Christ we are *more* than conquerors (Rom. 8:37). As children we had no greater source of credibility than the adults who influenced us. But as adults we can place our trust in a source of credibility that is greater than whatever or whoever installed lies in our minds—indeed, that is greater than *our own* minds (1 John 3:20). We can declare that God is true and that every dissenting voice in our lives is a lie (Rom. 3:4).

Many times adults give up hope of changing because even though they may know that dysfunctional or ungodly aspects of their lives are rooted in lies, these aspects of their experienced identity feel so permanent, so real, so huge. In this light, it helps to remember that there is no lie in your brain that is more than a microscopic electrical-chemical impulse. It's nothing more than a neural-net. My conviction that love meant pain felt so real, so unalterable, and so true. In fact, however, it was simply a microscopic chemical reaction in my misprogrammed brain.

So it is with every aspect of our lives that is out of sync with the truth of who we are in Christ. Our fear of love, our compulsiveness, our need to always be right, our inclination toward promiscuity, our need to control, our fear of food, our shame, and our insecurities—though they may have characterized us most of our lives—are nothing more than microscopic chemical reactions in our brains. The mental virtual-reality experiences that these reactions create feel so real and so permanent, and therein lies their power to deceive us. In truth they are each only an automated chemical reaction that is about a centimeter in size and a fraction of a second in duration. Most importantly, they can be altered. They must be altered, for no child of the King of Kings should be held captive by a microscopic, momentary, electrical-chemical charge.

Believe It or Not

It starts with a commitment to believe. If you want to be free to experience real life—the true *you*—you must *believe* that you are more than all the forces of causality that impact you. You must accept that you are not fated to be who you have experienced yourself to be up to this point. To escape the Matrix, you must resolve to believe that what God says about you is true *however much your past or present experience tells you otherwise*. However *real* the old *you* seems, you must accept that it is not *true*.

In other words, to transform our minds we must commit to ascribing more credibility to God than to our own brains. Our Matrix-conditioned brains are the problem; they therefore cannot be the foundation of the solution. We have to grasp hold of something that has more credibility than our own brains. We need to have a source of truth that doesn't depend on our own misprogrammed, organic computer. And this source can only be God's Word, centered on the person of Jesus Christ.

If you are to experience freedom, therefore, God's Word about your true identity in Christ must have more credibility to you than the word of parents, friends, other authorities in your life, and your own past and present experiences. But it's up to you. You are free to believe it or not. Will you choose the blue pill and go back to your *ordinary self* sleepily going through life as you are defined by all the past and present Matrix forces around you? Or will you take the red pill and see "how deep the rabbit hole goes"?

As Morpheus said to Neo, all we're offering "is the truth. Nothing more."

The True *You* in Christ

The truth we're asking you to believe—or rather, God is asking you to believe—is, in fact, almost unbelievable. Here's some of what the Bible says.[1] If you place your trust in Christ, God places you "in Christ" (e.g., Rom. 6:11; 8:1; 12:5; 1 Cor. 1:2; 15:22; Eph. 1:3–4). This means that everything that belongs to Christ by nature is shared with you by grace. This isn't nice poetry; it's factually true. You really are "in Christ"!

Being "in Christ" means:

- You share in Christ's abundant life, which is nothing less than the eternal life of the triune God (John 10:10; 2 Peter 1:4).
- You have the same perfect righteousness Christ has (2 Cor. 5:21).
- You are as dead to sin and as reconciled to God and as free from condemnation as Christ is (Rom. 3:24; 6:1–10; 8:1; 2 Cor. 5:19).
- You are heir of all the blessings to which Christ is heir (Eph. 1:4–11; 1 Peter 1:4).
- Though you once were "far away," you are now as near to God as Christ himself is (Eph. 2:13).
- You have the same Spirit of God, the same fearlessness, and the same love, joy, and peace that Christ himself has (John 15:11; 2 Cor. 5:14; Eph. 1:13; Phil. 4:7; 2 Tim. 1:7).

- *You couldn't be loved more than you are this very moment* because you are loved with the same perfect love the Father has for the Son (John 17:20–26).

- You now participate in the dance of the eternal triune God and are made a participant in the eternal divine nature (1 Peter 1:4).

And all this time you thought you were just an ordinary, church-going secretary or plumber! Instead you are a secretary "in Christ" or a plumber "in Christ." And this "in Christ" defines the true *you*. This isn't true about you because you earn it, experience it, or even fully believe it. It's true only because the loving and merciful God who is the Creator of all reality has *decided this is what's true about you*. His decree makes things real, and he has decreed this for you. When you are willing to submit to this truth, God speaks light into your life just as he spoke light into existence on the first day of creation (2 Cor. 4:6). And this is the light God has spoken into your being: you *really are* a new creation in Christ (2 Cor. 5:17).

The all-important question is: do *you* define yourself this way? Not just in principle—based on your heart surrendering to Jesus—but in the moment-by-moment experiences of your life? Which is to say, does the virtual-reality world you live in between your ears *agree* with the reality of Christ's lordship in your life, or does it *conflict with it?*

Doreen had surrendered her life to Christ and consciously knew who she was in Christ. But it did her no good when she came upon a beetle. In those moments Doreen's mischievous brother and a thirty-year-old memory were "lord" of her life. For, despite her profession of faith, they defined how Doreen experienced herself in those moments.

If our knowledge of who we are in Christ remains abstract, it will never be adequate to debug our brains of renegade neurochips. Our identity in Christ will never permeate our minds and become integrated into every area of our lives. We won't experience our true identity as real. For this to happen, we need to experience who we are in Christ as concretely and as vividly as we do our memories—or the beer commercials we watch.

The Brain Is Programmed by Events

It's vitally important to understand that the patterned electrical-chemical reactions in our brains that keep us from experiencing our true identity were installed by *events we experienced*. The brain records events and reactivates them—causing us to reexperience them—whenever it thinks they are significant for our interaction with our environment (that is, whenever triggered). It is our brains' built-in way of telling us to move toward something, to move away from something, to maintain something, to start something, or to stop something.[2]

This works as God intended when these reactivations produce positive feelings about things that are truly positive and negative feelings about things that are truly negative. But it works against us when the brain's programming is according to the pattern of this world. For now the brain produces positive feelings about things that are in truth negative and negative feelings about things that are in truth positive.

What is true of the brain's programming is also true of the brain's reprogramming: *it requires an event*. Conceptual information alone does not suffice. To get free from the Matrix, we have to fight according to the rules of the Matrix. But note, the events we are talking about are not necessarily events outside ourselves, experienced through our physical five senses. They can be events that are experienced within our brains.

What matters to the neurons in our brains is not whether an event is external or internal but only whether or not the event is experienced as *real, concrete,* and *vivid*. To debug renegade neurochips from our brains, therefore, we need to work with God to create events in our minds that communicate truth as vividly as our renegade neurochips communicate lies—as vivid as our memories and as graphic as the beer commercials we watch.

Creating Truth-Communicating Events

So how do we create truth-communicating events in our minds? The same way we created deception-communicating events in our minds. We create events in our minds by experiencing something in our minds as though it were real. We embody it with all five senses in a mental re-presentation. To create a truth-communicating event, therefore, we simply take a truth and embody it in our mental world with all five senses. We take a *truth* and mentally experience it as *real*.

For example, consider the truth mentioned earlier that you right now share in Christ's own life, love, joy, and peace. Ask yourself: What would I look like if this truth was perfectly integrated into my life? What thoughts would I have if this was perfectly true in my life? What would my feelings be like if this was perfectly true in my life? How would my thoughts, feelings, and behaviors differ from the ones I have now? Ask the Holy Spirit to give you a vivid, three-dimensional, re-presentation of this true *you*.

Don't just recite *information* about how you think you'd be different. *Get a picture* of yourself and see how you're different. *Listen* to how this God-glorifying *you* thinks and speaks differently from the way you presently tend to think and speak. *Observe* how you feel about things when you manifest the truth of who you are in Christ, and note how it's different from the way you presently tend to feel about those things. Don't just *know about* the true you; *experience* the true you.

Some readers may find it helpful to envision a split screen in their minds. On one screen, for example, see a time when you did anger inappropriately. On the other screen, envision how you would do this same event if you manifested the mind of Christ (Phil. 2:5). Notice how it looks, sounds, and feels to be in the same situation and have Christ's mind.

Once you've done this, step into the screen of the *you* that manifests the mind of Christ (associate to it). Think the thoughts, hear the sounds, and feel the feelings you have as you experience this way of responding to a difficult situation. Then remind yourself that on God's authority, *this* is who you truly are.

This is what a truth-communicating event in your mind looks, sounds, and feels like. The more like real life the truth-communicating re-presentation, the more impacting the event will be to you. Though most readers have probably never intentionally engaged in this sort of mental activity, we believe it is extremely important for spiritual growth. If we can't experience a truth in our minds, we can't hope to experience it in our lives. With

God's help, however, we can experience it in both. *For these truth-communicating events re-present who we really are.*

We encourage you to regularly take time out to create truth-communicating events of the sort we just reviewed in relation to every distinct aspect of who you are in Christ (see exercise 6 at end of chapter). When appropriate, imagine circumstances or a particular situation in which you manifest each of these truths *the least*—perhaps even where you tend to manifest the opposite of this truth. Watch yourself in each scene of the real *you*, and then become (associate to) the *you* of this scene. Experience it through your own eyes. And conclude each scene by saying, "On God's authority, *this* is the *true* me!"

Don't worry if it initially feels like you're pretending as you run these truth-communicating movies. As we noted in the previous chapter, when we contradict re-presentations we are used to assuming are true, it often feels like we're pretending. Here is where it becomes vitally important for you to affirm that God's Word about your identity in Christ has more credibility than anything you think or feel that conflicts with God's Word. On God's authority, the truth is that the *you* who doesn't manifest the truth of who you are in Christ is a pretense, however real it seems. And the *you* that you're re-presenting that does manifest the truth of who you are in Christ is the *true you*, however much like pretense it may initially seem. You've got to resolve in your mind that God is true, and any picture, word, or feeling that disagrees with this is lying (Rom. 3:4; 2 Cor. 10:3–5).

The Principle of Faith

Though the concept of a mental truth-communicating event undoubtedly sounds odd to some, all we are doing in creating such events is exercising faith that what God says about us is true. Whereas we were exercising faith that the Matrix-defined self we have always experienced as real was true, we are now exercising faith that the new self we have in Christ is true—which in turn is helping us experience it as *real*.

The Bible defines faith as "the assurance of things hoped for, the conviction of things not seen" (Heb. 11:1 NASB). We "do faith" by running previews in our minds of what we *expect* and by experiencing the conviction that this is what *will* come to pass. (Remember, all emotions, including feeling confident something will come to pass, are associated to mental re-presentations.) In fact, the word for *assurance* in this passage (*hypostasis*) literally means "substance" (and is translated as such in the KJV). We could apply this to mean that faith is the substantial reality—the concrete re-presentations—we hold in our minds that brings about the confident expectation that something will come to pass.

People often think that faith is only a *religious* thing. On the contrary, faith is a *life* thing. Faith is involved in everything we experience and everything we do. Jill had faith that made her completely certain God did not care about her. Under the right triggers, Doreen had faith that gave her the terrified conviction that she would be eaten by insects. Each re-presented something in their minds as real (*hypostasis*), and it produced a particular conviction about what to expect. Anyone who experienced what they experienced in their minds—anyone who had the faith they had—would feel abandoned by God or would fear insects. By the same means, anyone who has faith in God as revealed in Christ or faith that insects are mostly harmless will be free from the bondages Jill and Doreen experienced.

It's all about the content of our faith. The information we consciously believe is not nearly as important to the quality of our lives as the faith we hold as a substantial reality in our minds.

We see that when Jesus told the blind men, "According to your faith will it be done to you" (Matt. 9:29), he wasn't giving a religious formula; he was giving a universal life principle. All other things being equal, we tend to experience what we expect to experience. What we experience as real in our minds largely determines what we experience in our lives. Hence Scripture teaches that "as [a person] thinks within himself, so he is" (Prov. 23:7 NASB).

We are transformed by the renewing of our minds and transformed by our faith, for better or for worse. We become what we internally experience, for better or for worse (2 Cor. 3:17–4:6). When we create truth-communicating events in our minds, we are simply bringing our faith into alignment with truth. We are not engaging in wishful thinking—though our old self neuro-chips that are used to identifying lies as real may cause us to feel this way, at least at first. We are rather moving our minds in the direction of truth. We don't create who we are by thinking a certain way; that is what pop psychology tries to do. Instead, we are simply aligning our minds with truth to experience who we really are in Christ. We're removing the "splinter in our minds" by waking up to reality.

Smashing Pornography in the Mind

The point we're making was powerfully illustrated by a young man I (Al) counseled several years ago. As is happening at an alarming rate in America these days, Mark was addicted to pornography and had been so since he was a teenager. He came into counseling after his wife caught him masturbating while viewing Internet porn. Up to this point, Mark had managed to hide his secret addiction throughout the eight years of his marriage.

Mark was a thirty-three-year-old, successful man who was quite active in church. But porn addiction had been stealing, killing, and destroying his walk with God (John 10:10). He lived in shame and had often wondered whether he was really saved. Mark knew pornography was sinful, degrading, and destructive. Consistent with Jesus's teaching (Matt. 5:28), he considered it on a par with adultery. In fact, through his own reading, Mark even knew a good deal about what one should do to get free from pornography. It was for the most part good information. However, Mark remained in bondage—for his deep structure *faith* about pornography had never changed.

The first thing I did with Mark was to provide some teaching about how the brain works and about the principle of faith. On the basis of Hebrews 11:1, I explained that faith is about what we hold as a substantial reality in our minds associated to an emotion in our hearts that invariably leads to a particular outcome in our behavior. I didn't have to know any of the details about Mark's addiction to know that, despite his conscious beliefs to the contrary, Mark was in fact having faith that pornography was in some way a positive thing and that a part of him believed he needed it. Mark's behavior made this perfectly clear. Any normal male who experienced the substantial pictures, words, and sensations Mark experienced in his mind would in all likelihood engage in viewing pornography sooner or later.

Freedom is not about mustering up the willpower to abstain from doing something you want to do. Rather, freedom is not wanting to do it anymore, and this is all about the faith we hold. One cannot have faith that pornography or anything else is positive and not desire it. To change one's desire, one has to change one's faith.

It was time for Mark to bring his faith into alignment with his conscious beliefs about the evil of pornography. Our conversation went along these lines:

> **AL:** Mark, I want you to imagine your favorite pornographic scene.
>
> **MARK:** You're kidding! You *want* me to think of a pornographic scene?
>
> **AL:** Yes. But our purpose is not to enjoy it but to learn from it. We're going to teach your brain how to be free from wanting to view this material any longer. So go ahead, pull one up. Got it?
>
> **MARK:** Yes.
>
> **AL:** Is it a moving picture—a video—or is it a photograph?
>
> **MARK:** Well, it's a scene from a tape I recently watched. It's moving.
>
> **AL:** Okay. I want you to freeze-frame it. [*Mark nods when this is done.*] Now I want you to turn this image into glass and then smash it. Hear the glass break and see the pieces fall on the ground.
>
> **MARK:** Okay, I did that.
>
> **AL:** Now pull up another one, freeze-frame it, and smash it, just like the first. But this time when you smash it, say internally, "I am done with this garbage. I will not allow these pictures to keep me in bondage any longer."
>
> **MARK:** Interesting. This is honestly the first time I have ever felt I had some control over these pictures.
>
> **AL:** Great. Now, smash another pornographic picture and say with a loud, internal voice, "This is *my* brain and *I* determine

what I allow to be seen in here. God gave me authority over
my thoughts!"

MARK: Okay, that feels fantastic.

I then instructed Mark that any time he caught his brain
popping up memories of pornographic scenes, he was to immediately carry out this truth-communicating event. I was beginning to instruct Mark on how to change his faith—his internal
re-presentation—about his bondage to his addiction.

Learning What Men *Really* Want

Our conversation then continued.

AL: Now, Mark, I want you to remember your first exposure to
pornography. Tell me what comes to your mind when you
remember this event.

MARK: I was in our garage and I found some X-rated magazines that
my dad had hidden. So I started looking through them.

AL: Are you seeing this scene through your own eyes, or do you
see yourself in the memory?

MARK: I'm seeing it as if I was there, through my own eyes. I don't
see me.

AL: How old are you?

MARK: I'm fourteen or fifteen.

AL: Do you hear anything as you're looking at the magazine?

MARK: [*chuckles*] Actually, I do. I am hearing my thoughts, the
thoughts I had as a boy.

AL: What does the inner voice say?

MARK: I am saying to myself, "Wow, this is what men want." I
wanted to be like my dad. He always seemed so strong and
authoritative. I remember thinking that this would make me
a man and I would be like him.

AL: Excellent. What else do you know from what you are
remembering?

MARK: It felt wrong to me. I was surprised my dad had these. But it also felt like I had suddenly grown up. It felt like I had suddenly come of age or something. I remember thinking this would be my secret, my way of being like my dad. I actually stole his magazines, but he never confronted me about it. I think he was embarrassed.

AL: Anything else?

MARK: [*pausing a moment*] I don't know.

I asked Mark to pray with me and ask the Holy Spirit to help him learn about this area of his life. When we finished praying, I asked Mark to tell me what the Holy Spirit had given him.

MARK: I'm having a lot of pictures flash through my mind right now. I'm remembering many of the times I viewed pornography over the years. It seems they were usually times when I felt insecure or down. Sometimes I viewed them after I was criticized or when I was feeling vulnerable.

AL: Thank you, Mark. It is really good that you are willing to work through this. Now, Mark, how old are you again?

MARK: I'm thirty-three.

AL: You're not a teenager anymore, are you?

MARK: No.

AL: Your teenage voice said, "This is what men want." But I want you to challenge this voice as the informed adult that you are. Is this what men *really* want?

MARK: It certainly seems to be what a lot of men want!

AL: Think about your life and all you've learned since you were a teenager. From everything that you have learned, is this what most men *really* want? Even more importantly, think about the men you want to be like. Is it what they want? Think about the men you most admire. Do they really just want sex without love—sex with women they don't care about or even know? I will give you a little time to think about this.

MARK: [after a few minutes] No. I don't want that in my life. And I don't want that kind of sex. I had that once before I was married, and I honestly didn't like it at all. It left me feeling empty. I think that kind of sex always does.

AL: Okay, hear the teenage voice say again, "This is what men want." And when you do, tell the voice to stop. Tell the voice the truth that your thirty-three-year-old adult self knows. Men really don't want this kind of shallow sex, and you certainly don't want this kind of sex. Notice if anything occurs when you tell this to the teenage part of you.

MARK: I heard the voice say, "Okay," like I would have if someone had sat down and talked to me about it. I feel relieved.

AL: Great. Now, Mark, see the teenage you and know that the teenage you is watching and listening to us right now. Mark, I want you to know you're helping the teenage part of you grow up to know the truth. Okay, now blank the screen. Is it clear?

Now I want you to continue to teach the teenage neural-net about pornography. See one of the pornographic videos that you watched in the past. Can you see one?

MARK: All too easily.

AL: Okay, what I want you to do is ask Jesus to step into that video and notice what happens.

MARK: Jesus stepping into a porn video?

AL: He was in fact there, right? He knows about it. So just allow your mind to re-present this truth and notice what happens. I will pray for you as you do.

MARK: Wow. [laughing nervously]

AL: Tell me what you see.

MARK: Some of the actors run out of the scene. Others cover themselves up right away. They're ashamed of themselves. I can tell that they know what they're doing is wrong just by Jesus's presence.

AL: Mark, that is fantastic! It's essential for you to have the mind of Christ about pornography and about the destruction it creates in so many lives.

■ ■

Acquiring a *True* Faith about Pornography

AL: Now I'm going to pray, and as I do I want you to ask the Holy Spirit to reveal to you the truth about pornography. I want you to ask the Holy Spirit to reveal to you his thoughts and feelings about pornography. [*Almost immediately Mark became visibly distressed and began to cry.*] What are you experiencing, Mark?

MARK: I see gremlinlike demons all around the entrance of the sex store where I buy porn tapes. They're drooling and laughing at the men they're trapping. One has a ring in a man's nose and is pulling him into the store, but I can tell that the guy doesn't know it. Another man is gazing ahead mindlessly and walking like a robot.

AL: That's interesting, isn't it, Mark? This doesn't seem to be what men really want, does it? It's what Satan and his demons want.

MARK: The men are slaves.

AL: This may be difficult, but I believe there's more. I want you to take whatever time it takes for God to reveal his mind about "what men want" to you. I want you to experience the truth about pornography with the mind of Christ. Let's ask God to show you more. When we are finished, the meaning of pornography and the faith you have about pornography will be totally changed. You'll see it for what it really is. I'll pray. You just open your heart up to truth.

At this point Mark closed his eyes for about a minute. With each passing second he seemed to become more distressed and to sob harder and harder. Then he opened his bloodshot eyes.

Mark: It's terrible.

Al: Tell me exactly what you saw, heard, and felt.

Mark: First I was in the store. It was dim and smelly. I saw feces, blood, and vomit dripping from the videos and other sex merchandise. The demons were lapping it up and laughing. The men were blinded to it. Then I saw a montage of scenes!

Al: I want to hear about it.

Mark: Families being torn apart. I heard a director say, "Cut," and I saw women who had been in a porn movie crying. Others looked numb, even dead. Some were raging about their miserable lives, saying they were all alone, sad, and used. Then . . . then I heard a little girl's voice crying in the background, and I knew that the same kingdom that masterminds the adult porn industry masterminds child porn. And I realized . . . *I've been contributing to that!*

Al: This is how God sees it, because this is how it *really* is to him.[3]

Mark: No wonder it breaks his heart. At the end I saw this really odd scene. Jesus seemed like he was in a huddle with some men, like a football team. He asked the men to do a job with him by taking a stand and fighting with him against this evil—by fighting for the crying child. But when the men came out of the huddle they all walked over to the side of the demons, like they were friends, and joined their team! Their mascot was a terrified little girl in chains, dressed up like a prostitute. And I saw that I was one of those men!

I prayed again with Mark, thanking the Holy Spirit for revealing his thoughts to Mark. Then we continued.

Al: I want you to be confirmed about what you just saw, Mark. A study done by the Attorney General's Board on Missing and Exploited Children (1987) found that child porn was the most sought after and the most expensive kind of porn.

Thousands upon thousands of children—especially children from third-world countries—are sold or kidnapped into sexual slavery.

MARK: It's unthinkable.

AL: It is. *This* is the faith about pornography God wants you to embrace, Mark. Whenever you find yourself tempted to engage in porn, you have a very important choice to make. You can either let yourself be led by the nose by a demon and buy the illusion that "this is what men want," or you can see it as God sees it and have faith that what God says about pornography is true.

MARK: I see that.

AL: Whenever a temptation arises—and it will, Mark—immediately run the scene God just showed you. *Immediately!* The real choice is not to resist something you crave. The most fundamental choice is about what kind of faith you're going to have, for *this determines what you crave.* You will crave pornography or be revolted by pornography depending on how you re-present it in your mind—depending on what faith you hold about it.

This was a powerful truth-communicating event. It forever altered Mark's faith about pornography. My time with Mark ended with me leading him in a prayer of confession and repentance for his participation in the pornographic destruction of women, men, and children. As so many of us have, Mark experienced the beautiful forgiveness and cleansing that flows from Calvary. I then encouraged Mark to regularly run faith-scenarios of who he is in Christ—scenarios that include, when necessary, smashing pornographic scenes in his mind and/or recalling the vivid truth about porn God had revealed to him.

Mark was well on his way to experiencing the truth that a child of God need never remain in bondage to Matrix neurochips. He was on his way to experiencing his true identity in Christ.

Exercise 6

Exercising Faith in Your True Identity

The goal of this exercise is to help you develop truth-communicating events that re-present your true identity in Christ. In other words, it's designed to help you begin to choose to experience faith in who you really are.

Listed below are various aspects of your identity in Christ. You've seen these before in exercise 2. In that exercise we were helping you become a detective of your mind by simply noticing aspects of your inner world that are not in conformity to your true identity in Christ. You learned how to locate neurochips, and in this exercise we want to help you begin to debug your brain of those neurochips.

This exercise involves four steps. Take the time to do this exercise; the more time you put into it, the greater the possibility that you will learn how to renew your mind.

Step 1: Read each biblical truth listed below and ask the Holy Spirit to create a full-color, vivid movie of what you look, think, and feel like when you perfectly manifest the truth under consideration. Speak each verse to yourself slowly while the Holy Spirit gives you the faith that corresponds to its truth. Once you have a movie, see yourself in different real-life situations living out your true identity in Christ. Carefully notice how you think, feel, and act when you incarnate the truth of the verse(s) and how this differs from the way you presently think, feel, and act in those situations.

Step 2: Once you are able to see yourself living out the biblical truth you're considering, associate to it and experience it through your own eyes. Experience the thoughts, attitudes, feelings, and behavior of the true *you* in various situations from the inside.

Step 3: Once you've experienced the truth you're associated to for a while, adjust the submodality distinctions along the lines taught in exercise 3 (brighten the color, add or intensify sound, include kinesthetic elements, etc.). Preserve all alterations that intensify the feeling of this being real and omit all alterations that lessen this feeling. Record any observations you make about how you did faith most effectively. What submodality adjustments produced the surest faith conviction that *this is* the true you?

p 4: Once the re-presentation feels very real (above a seven one-to-ten scale), say to yourself in a loud internal voice, "On God's authority, *this is the true me!*"

Since our identity in Christ is foundational to all spiritual growth, we strongly suggest that you commit to practicing this exercise several times a day. You might pick out one or two truths that you concentrate on for a day. You can do this in your devotional time as well as any other time. When you're driving somewhere, for example, ask the Holy Spirit to show you what faith in your true identity in Christ looks like as it manifests the truth you're considering that day.

Don't be discouraged if creating faith movies in your mind is initially difficult. If you are persistent, you'll find that you get better at this. Related to this, you'll find that your actual thoughts, feelings, and behaviors in the outside world begin to manifest these truths. The ultimate goal, of course, is to make these faith re-presentations part of our brain's autopilot and thus make these biblical truths part of your experienced identity.

"Because of Jesus Christ . . ."

Biblical truth	What you see, hear, and feel when you exercised faith in these truths most effectively
I am filled with the peace and joy of God (John 14:27; Rom. 14:17).	
I am God's beloved child (John 1:12; Eph. 1:5).	
I am completely forgiven, perfectly righteous, and free from condemnation (Rom. 5:1; 1 Cor. 6:20; Eph. 1:7).	
I am God's glorious temple and am filled with his fullness (1 Cor. 6:19; Eph. 3:19).	

Biblical truth	What you see, hear, and feel when you exercised faith in these truths most effectively
I am holy and blameless (Eph. 1:4).	
I am the recipient of an eternal, infinitely rich inheritance (Eph. 1:11, 18; 1 Peter 1:4).	
I am inseparable from God's love and will never be abandoned (Matt. 28:20; Rom. 8:35–39).	
I am the beautiful bride of Christ who ravishes the heart of God (Song of Songs 4:1–15; 6:4–9; Eph. 5:25–32).	
I am one over whom the Lord rejoices, sings, and claps (Zeph. 3:17).	
I am one for whom the Lord throws a party (Luke 15:7–10).	
I am indwelled by a fearless Spirit of love and self-control (2 Tim. 1:7).	
I am more than a conqueror in all things (Rom. 8:37).	

7

The Kiss of Trinity

Experiencing Freedom to Love

TRINITY: Neo, I'm not afraid anymore. . . . You see, you can't be dead. You can't be, because I love you. You hear me? I love you. . . . Now get up.

———— ✦ ————

God is love. God's love was revealed among us in this way: God sent his only Son into the world so that we might live through him.

1 John 4:8–9 NRSV

The LORD God commanded the man, "You may freely eat of every tree of the garden; but of the tree of the knowledge of good and evil you shall not eat, for in the day that you eat of it you shall die."

Genesis 2:16–17 NRSV

Get ready; we're about to discover just how deep the rabbit hole goes. We've talked about the lie about God and the lie about ourselves that are foundational pillars to the Matrix. Now we're going to address the origin and center of the world that has been pulled over our eyes.

In the process, we're going to learn how to experience the freedom to love as God loves by learning how not to eat of the Tree of the Knowledge of Good and Evil. For the Matrix that blocks us from experiencing God's love, we shall see, is centered on this very tree.

The Forbidden Tree

You're probably familiar with the story. God set a man and a woman in a paradiselike garden. In the center of the garden were two trees, one that brought life while the other, which was forbidden, brought death. The forbidden tree was called the Tree of the Knowledge of Good and Evil. Things were presumably going along rather nicely until the crafty serpent showed up and enticed Adam and Eve to eat from this forbidden tree. The rest is history.

In this story we learn the origin and the structure of the Matrix—for the inspired story isn't just a fairy tale; *it's the story of each of our lives*. The Matrix originates from, and is structured around, the Tree of the Knowledge of Good and Evil. Eating from this tree is *the original sin*.

Here's a question that is as important as it is overlooked: why was the forbidden tree called the Tree of the Knowledge of Good and Evil? Isn't knowing good and evil a good thing? Wouldn't you have thought the tree would have been labeled the Tree of Evil, Debauchery, Deception, or something of the sort?

No, it's called the Tree of the Knowledge of Good and Evil, and understanding why this is so takes us to the heart of the world that has been pulled over our eyes. For eating from this tree blinds us to the most important, and most wonderful, aspect of the true world. It blocks us from the perfect love that is the reason for all creation.[1]

We'll come back to the mysterious forbidden tree later, but first we need to examine more closely the perfect love to which it blinds us.

An Incomprehensible Love

It was the love of Trinity in the movie *The Matrix* that resurrected Neo and finally empowered him to become the master of the Matrix. The movie isn't far from truth.

Not only was it the love of the triune God that raised Christ from the dead, it was the love of the Trinity that created the world in the first place and pursued humanity despite our rebellion and self-inflicted bondage to Satan. And it's the love of the Trinity that sent Christ into the world to die on our behalf and now works in each of our lives to reconcile us back to God and empower us to walk in Christ's resurrected life.

God is love, the Bible says (1 John 4:8). Love isn't just something God *does*; it's what God *is*. As Father, Son, and Holy Spirit, God is perfect, unsurpassable, infinitely intense, pure love. He is love that has no beginning, no end, and no limitation. God created the world as an expression of this perfect, triune love and for the purpose of inviting others into this perfect, triune love. Love is the reason why anything exists and the ultimate purpose for which everything exists.

The ultimate revelation of God's eternal love and the quintessential definition of love is the person of Jesus Christ. "We know love by this," John tells us, "that [Jesus] laid down his life for us" (1 John 3:16 NRSV). By offering up Jesus Christ for our redemption, God sacrificially ascribed unsurpassable worth to us, even though we were not worthy. *That* is perfect love. And this is why Jesus Christ's incarnation, life, and death reveal God. The love of the eternal Trinity is manifested in God's act of becoming a man and then becoming our sin on the cross of Calvary (2 Cor. 5:21). God crosses an infinite distance to become what is antithetical to himself—sin—in order to rescue rebellious human beings who couldn't deserve it less. *That* is unsurpassable love! *That* is God!

Sometimes Christians have heard the story so often it has become passé for them. Try to hear it as though you've never heard it before. It's truly breathtaking. The Creator of the universe loved you to the point of being willing to experience death and hell for you!

There is no greater gulf God could have crossed and no greater extreme to which God could have gone than for the all-holy God to become sin on Calvary for our salvation. This infinite *extremity* reveals the infinite *intensity* of the love God eternally is. If we comprehend this at all, we see that this love is incomprehensible. For it is love without limit, and we simply have no way of getting our minds around something that is limitless.

In revealing this incomprehensible love through Christ, the Trinity restored the original plan for creation. God's love reconciled sinners back to himself and in principle defeated the devil, who held us in bondage. In Christ, love has been enthroned once again. The kingdom of God has come. When we say *yes* to this kingdom, we are made citizens of this kingdom and are destined to be restored into the image of the one who is perfect love (Rom. 8:29; 2 Cor. 5:17; Eph. 2:19; Phil. 3:20). Indeed, as we have already seen, we are placed in Christ and are thereby made the recipients and the participants of the very same incomprehensible love that God has within himself as Father, Son, and Holy Spirit.

The All-Important and All-Encompassing Command

Since love is the purpose for everything, it shouldn't surprise us to find that throughout the New Testament, manifesting God's love is presented as the single most important goal of our lives. Because we are in Christ, we are commanded to love as those who are loved in Christ. Hence, immediately after John told us that we know love by the fact that Christ "laid down his life for us," he added, "and we ought to lay down our lives for one another" (1 John 3:16 NRSV). We are called to be nothing less than imitators of Jesus Christ, willing to lay down our lives for others (Eph. 5:1–2; 1 Peter 2:21). We are, in other words, called to model God's incomprehensible love to all people.

This radical love is the central thing that is supposed to distinguish Jesus's disciples from "the world." It's not primarily our knowledge, our clever arguments, our spotless lives, our true beliefs, or our nice church buildings that God relies on to convince the world that Jesus is Lord; *it's our love*. When we love as God loves—when we love with an unconditional, self-sacrificial, Calvary-type love—people *see* that God is real and that Jesus Christ is Lord (John 13:35; 17:23).

Along with loving God with every ounce of our being, the command to love our neighbor is the greatest command, according to Jesus (Matt. 22:37–39). In fact, Scripture teaches that we can't genuinely love God and *not* love our neighbor (1 John 4:20). Paul and Peter taught us that the command to love is above all other commands (Col. 3:14; 1 Peter 4:8). If we fulfill this command, we fulfill all commands (Matt. 22:40; Rom. 13:8; Gal. 5:14; James 2:8). Conversely, Paul taught that if we don't love, it doesn't matter what else we do; *it's worthless*. We can speak in tongues, prophesy, have all knowledge, understand all mysteries, and even engage in every variety of good works, but if these activities are not motivated by love with the goal of furthering love, Paul says, they amount to nothing more than obnoxious, religious noise (1 Cor. 13:1–3).

Love is the all-or-nothing of the Christian life. Ultimately, it's the only thing that matters (Gal. 5:6). *Everything* we do is to be done in love (1 Cor. 16:14). If we can't engage in an activity out of love, we shouldn't do it. Being "right" in a theological debate, for example, is worthless to the extent that our motivation is to win more than it is to express love.

Along the same lines, the New Testament teaches that disciples are to imitate God by living in love and clothing ourselves with love at all times (Eph. 5:1–2; Col. 3:14). We are to love our enemies as well as our friends (Matt. 5:43–44; Luke 6:28, 35). We are never to return evil with evil but "overcome evil with good" (Rom. 12:21). We are to "be merciful, just as [our] Father is merciful" (Luke 6:36). God shows no partiality in the way he loves, and neither must we (Deut. 10:17–19; 2 Chron. 19:7; Mark 12:14; John 3:16; Acts 10:34; Rom. 2:10–11; Eph. 6:9; see also 1 Tim. 2:4; 1 Peter 1:17; 2 Peter 3:9). We are to regard anyone we come upon who is in need as a "neighbor" whom we are called to love, whether or not we think he or she deserves it (Luke 10:27–37). Out of love, we are to give to beggars, lend to those in need, and give without expecting anything in return (e.g., Matt. 5:39–42; Luke 6:31–36).

In other words, we are commanded and empowered to love without strings attached, without conditions, without any consideration whatsoever of the apparent worthiness of the person we encounter. We are commanded and empowered to love as God loves.

Loving like this is synonymous with life and joy, for it is the reason we were created. When we love like this, we experience the deepest, truest aspect of God, ourselves, and all other people. Loving like this is what it means to be a participant in the kingdom of God and in his divine nature (2 Peter 1:4). Loving like this is dancing within the intimate circle of the triune fellowship.

Have you ever had the experience of standing in a crowd of strangers and being so full of love you thought you were going to explode? It happens infrequently to me (Greg), but it does happen. The experience is simply indescribable. It is nothing short of ecstasy. In those moments I fully experience what it is to live in Christ and to walk in the Spirit. In those moments I feel enveloped within the eternal life, joy, and peace of the Trinity. In those moments I experience the purpose for which God created me and all other humans. In those moments I am kissed by the Trinity—and I experience resurrected life.

But let's be honest. None of us love like this with any degree of consistency. Our lives are mostly centered on ourselves, are they not? We perhaps love those close to us, but not people who treat us poorly. We perhaps love those we think deserve it, but not so much those we think are unworthy. Jesus attracted and spent most of his time with people whom society as a whole, and especially "religious" society, thought were unworthy—the prostitutes, the tax collectors, and other "sinners" (Matt. 9:10; Luke 5:29–30; 7:34; 15:1). But if we are honest, we will have to admit that these sorts of people aren't normally attracted to us individually or to the churches we attend—for we do not generally love as Jesus loved.

Whatever other reputation Christians may have, people aren't becoming convinced en masse that Jesus is the true Lord because of our outrageous love. Why is this? And what can we do about it? If we are in fact new creations in Christ Jesus who are filled with God's love, why is this not being manifested? If we diagnose our problem merely as a lack of effort on our part, we will completely miss the real issue and will find we make little progress toward loving as God loves. We'll just hand out more "supposed to's," which we know do little or no good.

No, as with all significant problems in our lives, the problem is much deeper than what our knowledge or willpower can address. The problem is the Matrix. The problem is that we are not yet free from the crafty deception of an Architect who ceaselessly works to steal and destroy the abundant life Christ has brought into the world (John 10:10).

And now we're ready to begin to understand why the forbidden tree was called the Tree of the Knowledge of Good and Evil.

Loving a Child Abuser

Let me (Greg) start with an illustration. Some time ago our local news station reported the death of a beautiful, three-year-old boy from wounds inflicted by his mother's live-in boyfriend. In fact, it turns out the child had been tortured in unthinkable ways by this brute almost since the day of his birth. His short life had been one prolonged, unimaginable nightmare.

I became enraged when I heard this news. No, I became *hateful*. I didn't only detest what happened to this boy; I despised the man who did this to him. A part of me not only wanted justice for the boy; I personally longed for vengeance against the man. Though I didn't admit this out loud or even to myself (I knew better), I have to confess that a part of me would have enjoyed seeing this man in hell. In fact—and most repugnantly—this part of me felt *righteous* for wanting this!

Later that night as I prayed, I suddenly got a picture in my mind of a badly beaten toddler locked in a dark closet trying to say something through loud, convulsing sobs. Terrified of the dark and hurting from his beating, the battered boy was begging an adult on the other side of the closet doors to let him out while promising "to be good." This vivid mental scene broke my heart with compassion and enraged me toward the boy's abuser.

But it also confused me. For I got the distinct impression I was supposed to pray for this boy I was envisaging in my mind. *What was I supposed to pray about?* I wondered. The boy was already dead.

Then in my mind I heard a distinct voice with a jarring message: "This boy is not the one who died; *he's the man who killed him*. Pray for *him*. Have compassion *on him*."

Talk about turning the tables!

I'm not certain the mental picture and message I received was a bona fide "message of knowledge" (1 Cor. 12:8) of what actually happened to the abuser as a child. It may have been. Or it may be that God just gave me this picture as a means of confronting my judgmentalism. But it really doesn't matter. The message served to wake me up to *what I didn't know*.

In truth, I *didn't know* anything about the history of this man I was despising. The message forced on me questions like: What happened to this man as a little boy? What made him into the monster he turned out to be? How did he learn to be so cruel? What was his childhood like? Was he himself born into a world that was a prolonged nightmare? How could a wonderful creation of God turn out so tragically?

No healthy and happy person just wakes up deciding to torture little children. This abusive man was once a tender little baby, once a boy who perhaps dreamed of being a baseball star—once was normal. Who killed, stole, and destroyed the life he could have and should have had (John 10:10)?

Whatever happened to this man in the past to help fashion him into a child-killer does not in any way diminish the horrifying evil of what he did. Nor does it imply that society shouldn't hold him morally responsible for this boy's suffering and death. For the sake of justice and for the good of society, this man must be locked up.

But the picture and the message I received clearly drove home one all-important truth: namely, *neither I nor any other human knows what only God knows*. Neither I nor any other human knows the extent to which this man freely chose to become a monster out of the morally responsible center of his being or the extent to which he himself was a victim of evil that was perpetrated on him. Genetic influences as well as spiritual and environmental influences are always mixed together with free will in people in ways that only God can untangle.

The one thing we *do* know—or at least should know—is that this man has unsurpassable worth before God, for Jesus paid an unsurpassable price for him. Thus, the only thing we know—or should know—is that our primary job as disciples of Jesus Christ is *to agree with God about this.*

Again, to protect itself, society must lock up this man. But those who are in Christ are commanded and empowered to go beyond social necessities and to actually love people like this—our "enemies"—with the love of Jesus Christ. We are called to do nothing less than imitate Jesus toward people like this. We are called to love to the point of being willing to lay down our lives on behalf of people like this, for this is exactly what Jesus did for us.

Whatever ultimate vengeance is to be exacted on this child-killer, on people like him, and on every other person is for God alone to decide. "Vengeance is mine, I will repay, says the Lord" (Rom. 12:19 NRSV; see also Deut. 32:35; Heb. 10:30). Hence the Bible consistently teaches that God alone is the judge of all the earth (e.g., James 4:11–12). As humans, our one and only job is to love—even when we at the same time must put one we love behind bars for the sake of others we love.

The picture I received of the boy in the closet broke the chains of judgment I harbored toward the abuser. It empowered me to surrender the searing animosity I had toward this man. And when I did this, something truly remarkable happened. I found myself moved with a profound, compassionate love for this man. Of course I was still sickened by what he did. And of course I still grieved for the abused boy's horrid life and death. But I was able to see beyond this man's behavior and to agree with God that this man was worth dying for.

Neither he nor I are worthy of Christ. But both he and I have worth—unsurpassable worth—because of Christ. Perhaps even more remarkable, when I surrendered my judgment, I experienced a certain level of joy in loving this "monster." I felt fully alive in loving the unlovable. And I felt profoundly close to God. I was being kissed by the Trinity once again.

When we cease trying to know what God alone knows in terms of judgment, we begin to know what God knows in terms of people's worth. We begin to love. And this means we begin to experience real life in Christ. Indeed, being able to love like Christ is the essence of our life in Christ.

■ ■
Blinded by a Tree

What had blocked me from loving the abusive man—and had therefore blocked me from being fully alive as a human in relation to him—was my judgment. I was playing God. I was acting as if it was my business to draw ultimate conclusions not just about this man's behavior but about the man himself. I was acting as though I knew ultimate good and evil: I, of course, was *good*, and this man, of course, was *evil*.

So long as I sat on my self-appointed throne of judgment and persisted in the Matrix illusion that I possessed omniscient knowledge about this man, I could not love him as Christ loved me. For I was eating from the Tree of the Knowledge of Good and Evil. Though we are deceived into thinking the tree *opens* our eyes (Gen. 3:5), the tree actually blinds us. It blinds us from seeing the most important thing: the unconditional worth God ascribes to us and all other people.

If we are faithful detectives of our own brains, we will soon discover that we eat from this forbidden tree *all the time*! What happened to me with regard to the child-killer happens to some extent to most of us each day. *We play God.* And this is why we fail to love as Christ loves.

Instead of viewing people in the light of Calvary, we tend to view them in the light of our opinions. Rather than ascribing unsurpassable worth to each individual we encounter, we tend to ascribe only whatever worth we at the moment want to give them. We tend to view people through filters of our own assessments, valuations, preferences, and judgments—our own knowledge of good and evil.

What we see when wearing these spectacles is not the infinite worth of people but whether or not they are good or evil, fat or skinny, pretty or ugly, right or wrong, godly or ungodly, wealthy or poor, gay or straight, religious or nonreligious—or a million other things. In a fraction of a second we label, stereotype, and file people according to our preset Matrix filters. We are strapped with automatically activated conclusions about almost everybody and everything. Instead of triggering a reminder to love unconditionally as we've been loved, seeing various types of people triggers neurochips of judgment. And every single one of these judgments conditions, if not blocks, the fathomless love of God flowing through us toward others. Each one serves to enslave us and keep us from being fully alive human beings. Each one anchors us in the Matrix.

The Provision and the Prohibition

With each one of these love-blocking judgments, we are replaying in our own lives the Genesis story of the fall of humanity. We are replicating the origin and reinforcing the structure of the Matrix. It's vitally important we understand this.

Like everything else God does, he placed the forbidden tree at the center of the Garden of Eden out of love. It was, if you will, God's loving "No Trespassing" sign. It was placed in the middle of the garden along with the Tree of Life to remind us that human life as God intends it is to be centered on two things. We are to trust God for his provision (the Tree of Life), on the one hand, and honor God's prohibition (the Tree of the Knowledge of Good and Evil), on the other. God was in effect telling us that living in the paradise he wants for us is predicated on our remembering that we are humans, not God. "Trust me for life," God was saying, "and don't try to be me."

The serpent tempted Eve by holding out the carrot of being like God (Gen. 3:5), yet the Bible says Adam and Eve were already in the image of God (Gen. 1:26–27). What the narrative suggests is that there is a legitimate and illegitimate way in which we are to be "like God." We are made to be in the image of God's love but not in the image of God's *knowledge*. We are to love as God loves but not know as God knows and therefore not judge as God judges. Love and judgment are for humans antithetical activities.

Tragically, Adam and Eve accepted a lie about God (see chapter 5) and thus accepted a lie about themselves (see chapter 6). Because of this deception, they believed that being like God in their capacity to receive and reflect God's life and love was not enough. If their eyes were to be opened, and if they were to realize their full potential, the serpent suggested that they needed to strive to also be like God in their capacity to know. They thus ate of the forbidden Tree of the Knowledge of Good and Evil. The Matrix came into being.

When Adam and Eve violated God's loving "No Trespassing" sign, they became judges rather than lovers. Instead of living out of the fullness of life and love God offered them for free, they began to live out of an emptiness they would have to try to fill by their own striving. Instead of manifesting the loving character of their Creator, they began manifesting the judging character of the Accuser who brought them under his dominion (Rev. 12:10). Thus, when God showed up, the humans immediately judged that he would be unmerciful, so they hid (Gen. 3:8). And when they were interviewed about what happened, Adam instinctively blamed Eve, and Eve instinctively blamed the serpent (Gen. 3:12–13).

And humans have been mistrusting God, deflecting responsibility, and judging each other ever since. We have become conformed to the image of the crafty serpent. We've learned how to employ the Tree of the Knowledge of Good and Evil to our own advantage. We've learned how to survive without love. But what we call "surviving," God calls "death" (Gen. 2:17).

Like the humans imprisoned in pods in the movie *The Matrix*, we think we are living, but we're not. Nothing is more fundamental to the Matrix of this world than this web of lies and the death-survival strategies it produces.

Feeding Ourselves with Condemnation

Let's go a little farther down the rabbit hole. Every behavior—including the behavior of thinking—serves some purpose in our lives. So let's ask, what purpose does our multitude of judgments about people serve?

There are times when we need to be discerning about people's character and behavior as well as the impact certain behaviors have. The purpose of this sort of legitimate mental behavior is to be wise in our interactions with others and in our own actions. If someone is trying to sell us a car or apply for a job, for example, we need to discern something about his or her character. And of course we need to be able to discern healthy and helpful behavior from unhealthy and harmful behavior. Indeed, the author of Hebrews instructs us to be mature in discerning good from evil in this sense (Heb. 5:14).

This wise discernment is not the judgment of condemnation that the Bible uniformly forbids, however. For discernment distinguishes one thing from another; but condemnation separates us from the person we judge. In condemningly judging others we stand apart from them and above them. You can agree with God that a person has unsurpassable worth even though you wouldn't buy a car from him or her. But you cannot agree with God and ascribe unsurpassable worth to a person while you're drawing ultimate conclusions about his or her inherent lack of worth.

My conviction that the man who killed the young boy did a terrible thing was discernment. My conclusion that he was evil and should burn in hell was condemnation. One straightforward way of perceiving the difference between these two is that discernment doesn't activate personal, negative feelings toward another while condemnation always does.

If we're honest and careful detectives of our brains, we'll discover that we often run commentaries in our minds about people that have nothing to do with a need to be wisely discerning. Rather, we will discover that we are condemning people instead of loving them. We are *detracting* worth from them rather than *ascribing* worth. And, if we examine ourselves closely, we will discover that we detract worth as a means of ascribing worth *to ourselves*. Like Adam and Eve, we condemn *as a strategy for getting life*.

Think of the last time your internal voice spoke words such as "That person is disgusting," "What a pervert," "What a hypocrite," "She thinks she's something," "What a slob," "whore," "idiot." What function does this internal gossip serve? It's a behavior God repeatedly forbids, yet we do it. Why? Is it not because we get a sense of worth and power by talking to ourselves this way? Doesn't it make us feel superior to pretend that others stand or fall before the tribunal of our own minds? Do we not on some level *enjoy* drawing negative conclusions about people? Though the Bible repeatedly forbids speaking evil of others (e.g., Matt. 5:22; 15:18–19; 1 Cor. 6:10; 2 Cor. 12:20; Titus 2:3; 3:2; James 4:11; 1 Peter 2:1), we enjoy and subtly feed off of speaking evil about people, at least to ourselves if not to other people. We like thinking we know "the truth" about others. *We like playing God!*

I felt *righteous* for standing over and above the abusive child-killer. And *that* is precisely why I stood there. However imperfect I may be, I thought, at least I was not like *that* child-abusing monster. In fact, my "righteous" animosity toward the abuser served as conclusive proof of just how different I was from him. So long as I could position myself in a morally superior position to this man and contrast myself with him, I didn't have to feel so bad about my own multitude of shortcomings. (This explains why fervently religious people are often angry at "the world" and so judgmental.) By focusing on this man's sin, I could deflect my attention off my own sin. And if I had expressed my condemnations out loud, I could have deflected others' attention as well, making us both feel righteous for not being like the abuser.

Yet the fact of the matter is that all the time we contrast ourselves with the abuser, we *are sinning*. We feast off our own version of the Tree of the Knowledge of Good and Evil. We thereby prevent ourselves from fulfilling the most fundamental responsibility God gave to us as Christians, namely, to love this man, and all people, with a Calvary-type unconditional love. We forget that we are mere humans—and fallen humans at that. We forget that we are not God.

If we are to be free to love as God loves, the Matrix accuser inside us must be taken captive.

Tree Trunks and Dust Particles

To help keep us from feasting off our judgments and to help us remain focused on our one responsibility as humans, Jesus taught us to do the *exact opposite* of what we do when we condemn a child abuser. Instead of trying to experience worth by minimizing our sin and magnifying the sin of others, Jesus taught us to get our worth totally from God while recognizing that we are all sinners. Indeed, he taught us to consider the sins of others—*whatever* they may be—to be little dust particles while considering *our own sin* to be tree trunks in our eyes (Matt. 7:1–3).

Of course, in terms of social consequences, child abuse must be deemed much worse than, for example, my lustful thoughts or your tendency to gossip or someone else's homosexual orientation or another person's addiction to food. But a disciple of Jesus must never equate the necessities of social evaluations and gradations with truth itself. The truth is that *all of us sin* (Rom. 3:23; 1 John 1:8). Some may sin in more socially destructive ways than others, but in terms of its power to separate us from God, sin is all one and the same.

Whether you "merely" speak disparagingly of another or actually murder (Matt. 5:21–22; 12:36), whether you "merely" think adulterous thoughts in your mind or actually engage in adultery (Matt. 5:27–28), Jesus says you deserve to be punished by being separated from God. In terms of our relationship with God—the one who alone defines ultimate truth—we are all sinners.

This is why Jesus emphasizes that we are in no position to judge others. We don't judge accurately because we are non-omniscient humans who can't know all the factors that lie behind a person's behavior. And we can't judge accurately because we have tree trunks of sin blocking our vision! Only God is truly good and holy (e.g., Matt. 19:17). Only God can see the heart and can judge accurately (e.g., 1 Sam. 16:7). Only God knows the ultimate truth about good and evil. Only God is the judge of the earth. While we must in love discern and sometimes take social measures to stop destructive behaviors, we must never pretend to "be like God, knowing good and evil" (Gen. 3:5).

We are called to be merely humans who get their innermost needs met by God. As mere humans, the only thing we can know, and the only thing we are supposed to know, is that every human being has infinite worth before his or her Creator. And our main task in life is to agree with God about this fact. We do this when we love as God loves. It makes no difference whether the person is a Mother Teresa or a murderer when it comes to our fulfilling this all-important and all-encompassing command.

Thou Shall Not Judge

The rest of the New Testament agrees with Jesus's teaching about judgment—which is to be expected, for it agrees with Jesus's teaching about the centrality of love. And as we have seen, these are two sides of the same coin.

For example, Paul sternly rebuked those who judged others, for in doing this they were forgetting that they were themselves sinners who stood before God only by his mercy (Rom. 2:1–4). In light of Paul's teaching, we must take every measure to avoid the common religious game of sanctioning certain sins—the ones we tend to commit—while coming down on other sins—the sins of "the world." When we play God and have others stand before our self-constructed and self-serving tribunal of justice, we always bend the criteria of good and evil in our favor. We are feasting on our own religious version of the Tree of the Knowledge of Good and Evil.

When we stand before the tribunal of God's justice, however, we are all equally condemned. There is, therefore, nothing to be gained and much to be lost by contrasting ourselves with others. Our one job is to love, and the one thing that will prevent us from doing this is our tendency to judge others. Another way of saying this is that eating from the Tree of the Knowledge of Good and Evil is the thing that bans us from the Tree of Life (Gen. 3:22–24).

Paul addressed the issue of judgment in another place when he wrote: "Who are you to pass judgment on servants of another? It is before their own lord that they stand or fall" (Rom. 14:4 NRSV; see also verse 10). Servants are accountable only to the "lord" who hired them (or, in Paul's day, who purchased them). Before this one alone do they "stand or fall." So too, Paul says, we each must answer to the Lord Jesus Christ who gave his life for us (vv. 12, 22–23). When we judge others, even in our own minds, we are acting as though they are accountable *to us*. We are acting as though we are their "lord." We are playing God.

In contrast to this, Paul reiterates that our one and only task is to concern ourselves with whether we are doing what the Lord requires of us and whether we are acting in ways that honor the worth of all others before God (Rom. 14:3, 5–7, 13, 15). We are called to walk in love, not judgment.

James drives home this same point when he writes: "Whoever speaks evil against another or judges another, speaks evil against the law and judges the law; but if you judge the law, you are not a doer of the law but a judge. There is one lawgiver and judge who is able to save and to destroy. So who, then, are you to judge your neighbor?" (James 4:11–12 NRSV).

As we have seen, the essence of the law is to love. This is why James elsewhere calls it "the royal law" (James 2:8). When we go beyond this and judge another in word or thought, we are not doing the law. We are, in fact, judging the law. For we are acting as though we are the law—as though God and the law weren't adequate to hold people accountable. We are not trusting that "the Judge of all the earth [will] do what is just" (Gen. 18:25 NRSV).

To prevent this, James reminds us that there is one lawgiver and judge who will do what is just. He reminds us that we are trying to usurp God's throne when we speak evil or judge another. And he reminds us that our one job as humans is to do the law—to ascribe to all people the worth God ascribes to them in dying for them on Calvary—and leave to God the task that only an omniscient being can do, namely, judge humans accurately.

The Forbidden Tree and the Matrix

All of these (and other) passages about judgment are simply various ways of reiterating the divine prohibition as a means of restoring to us the divine provision. "You shall not eat of the fruit of the tree that is in the middle of the garden" (Gen. 3:3 NRSV); "Do not judge" (Matt. 7:1); you shall love and forgive as you have been loved and have been forgiven (Luke 6:36–38). These commands are inseparably connected. In fact, they are different facets of the same truth, and they each cut to the core of the Matrix.

Insofar as we are conformed to the unreal world of the Matrix, we instantly assess people and things as *good* or *evil* depending on what they do for us. And what we think is good or evil for us depends on what we are trying to get life from. For example, if we happen to be trying to get our worth and security from a religious idol, then people and things that make us feel holy, that reaffirm the correctness of our beliefs, and that make us feel different from "those sinners" will be judged as good. And our judgment that (in our own mind) separates us from "those sinners" will be judged as good. Conversely, people and things that contrast with our supposed "holiness" as well as things that confront our beliefs or make us feel far from God will be deemed evil.

If, however, we are trying to get our worth and security from a secular idol—for example, the idol of wealth—then people and things that make us look and feel wealthy will be deemed good, and those that contrast with and/or detract from our wealth will be deemed evil. Though religious idols look better than secular ones—at least in the eyes of other religious people—they are equally aspects of the Matrix.

We each bend the Tree of the Knowledge of Good and Evil in our own unique way so we can feed off it, but it's the same forbidden Tree. What's more, we're trapped in a vicious cycle, a Catch-22. The enemy who seeks to kill, steal, and destroy the abundant life God intends for us is crafty indeed (John 10:10). For eating from the forbidden tree is not only *the result* of our not getting full life from God, it's *the cause* of our not getting full life from God. We eat because we are empty, and we're empty because we eat.

The definition of this sort of self-sustaining cycle is addiction, and it's utterly diabolical. For, in fact, it is the main thing that keeps us from God's abundant life as well as the main evidence that we are kept from God's abundant life. Which is to say, it is the main thing that keeps us entrapped in the Matrix as well as the main evidence that we are trapped within the Matrix.

The exercise that follows can help us break this cycle of addiction and begin to set our minds free to experience real life in Christ—the life of outrageous love.

Exercise 7

Silencing the Judger and Releasing the Lover

Exercise 7 will help us learn how to abstain from original sin and therefore release God's unconditional love in our lives. A preliminary word must first be said, however.

The fundamental driving force behind our condemnation of others is a felt lack of worth, significance, and security in ourselves. In one form or another, we feel empty and insecure, and we judge others as a way of trying to get full. This is true whether we are judging with a religious or secular mindset. The ultimate reason we feel empty or insecure is because we are not experiencing fullness of life out of our relationship with Christ because we yet experience Matrix misre-presentations of God and ourselves.

The key to being set free to reflect God's unconditional love to others, therefore, is to have *true* re-presentations of God and of ourselves. We can only give love unconditionally if we are consistently experiencing unconditional love. Thus, before offering exercise 7, we want to remind you to be persistent in practicing exercises 5 and 6, which address these issues.

Exercise 7 is designed to help us collapse our judger—the part of us that eats from the Tree of the Knowledge of Good and Evil—in order to extend God's love to others. This exercise has two distinct applications, one to be done alone and the other to be done in public.

Application 1: Get alone and bring before your mind re-presentations of various people you are most inclined to judge. Think of specific individuals or re-presentations of types that you tend to think are evil, disgusting, immoral, etc. Then, as you're holding the re-presentation in mind, ask God to give you his Calvary love for this person. Say in your internal voice, "I agree with God that this person has unsurpassable worth, for Christ thought him/her worth dying for." Remind yourself that your most fundamental job in life is to simply agree with God about the worth of all individuals. Notice if this strategy alters your re-presentation of the person and/or your feelings about this person.

As God did with me regarding the child abuser, you might ask God to help you imagine a story that explains what might be motivating this person to be the way he or she is—a story that elicits compassion rather than judgment. The story need not be factual, for its purpose is simply to remind you of all that you do not know about the person you're judging.

Finally, speak to the judger part of yourself and thank it for reminding you that your job as a fellow fallen human being is to love as you've been loved, not judge as only God can judge. Then, using the truths given in exercise 6, remind your soul who you *really* are in Christ and that you don't need to scrape up morsels of worth by taking it from others.

Application 2: All mental discipleship—being transformed by the renewing of our minds—is about bringing to conscious awareness mental behavior that is so fast it usually resides below the conscious level. As it concerns love, it's about bringing before our conscious awareness the verbal, visual, or kinesthetic message-laden images our Matrix-polluted brains automatically display in response to various people we see or encounter. It's about ending our addiction to the Tree of the Knowledge of Good and Evil.

To this end, it will help to set aside an hour or two once a week or so to go to a busy, public place for the sole purpose of noticing what internal dialogue naturally occurs in response to the various people you see. When you notice a negative internal commentary starting or negative mental re-presentations aris-ing in reaction to various individuals, immediately *thank* the part of you that was judging others for reminding you of your central job in life. Tell it that from now on its job is to remind you that you are commissioned by God to love all people at all times in all places without exception. Tell it that from now on, any judgmental message, verbal or otherwise, will serve as a reminder to love as God loves. Then agree with God and ascribe unsurpassable worth to the person you caught yourself judging. You might simply say, "I agree with God that this person has unsurpassable worth because of Jesus Christ. Thank you, God, for creating him/her and for dying for him/her." End with a quick prayer of blessing for the person, however God leads you.

Some may find it helpful to visually re-present the worth God ascribes to people as you ascribe worth to them. You can do this with actual people you encounter or simply as a mental exercise alone. I (Greg) often envision a warm violet glow around people re-presenting the radiant love of God that envelops them, whether they know it or not. Some readers may feel this is corny, but any way we can concretely re-present truth is helpful. If you're like me, you'll find it tends to reinforce the sense that the worth these people have is real, not fictitious.

As I say these words and re-present this glow, I sometimes feel a release of love toward them. Indeed, I am finding that, though it is still rather rare, I am increasingly experiencing a profound love and compassion for people—especially the ones who by society's customary "knowledge of good and evil" would be far on the evil side of things. And in a few instances, as I've said above, I feel as though I'm going to explode with joy. I feel resurrected by the kiss of the Trinity. This is the essence of ex-periencing real life in Christ.

8

Matrix Revolutions

Overcoming Wounding Memories

MORPHEUS: I'm trying to free your mind, Neo, but I can only show you the door. You're the one that has to walk through it. . . . You have to let it all go, Neo: fear, doubt, and disbelief. Free your mind.

———∞∞———

It is the LORD who goes before you. He will be with you; he will not fail you or forsake you. Do not fear or be dismayed.

Deuteronomy 31:8 NRSV

It is for freedom that Christ has set us free. Stand firm, then, and do not let yourselves be burdened again by a yoke of slavery.

Galatians 5:1

Frozen in Time

Agent Smith begins to take on a life of his own in *The Matrix Reloaded*. He discovers autonomy. He becomes something of a computer virus that is no longer integrated within the context of the computer-generated Matrix. As such, he becomes increasingly destructive.

Many of our most debilitating neurochips act like this. We experience a traumatic event at some point in our lives and a part of us becomes frozen in that event. The neural-net that encodes this event operates on autopilot whenever triggered. In a fraction of a second it re-presents the event in a concrete, experiential fashion. And it does so from the perspective—and with the emotional meaning—we had when we originally experienced the event. While the rest of our self has moved on, *this part of us did not*. It is frozen in time, as it were. It is autonomous.

For this reason, whenever we encounter triggers that activate this neural-net, we do not respond in ways that reflect our overall maturity level. Rather, when we are experiencing the world from the perspective of this neural-net, we only have the resources that were available to us when the neural-net was first installed. If the neural-net was created when we were seven, we emotionally become a seven-year-old when it is triggered. We thus respond with the maturity level of a seven-year-old.

If you have ever wondered why you continue to respond to certain situations in immature and nonproductive ways, we suggest you become a detective of your mind and look for parts of yourself that are frozen in time and are triggered in these particular situations. All of us have frozen areas like this; they are Matrix neurochips. Under the right conditions, we experience feelings such as lust, anger, jealousy, selfishness, or fear that are out of character with the rest of our lives. Frozen-in-time re-presentations are activated, and we emotionally become the age at which we were frozen.

At several points throughout this book we have mentioned Doreen, the woman who had a profound phobia about insects. She poignantly illustrates how profoundly we can be frozen. It's now time to see how Doreen was set free from her thirty-year-old fear. In the process we will discover a technique that can help each of us, as Morpheus said, let go of fear, doubt, and disbelief and free our minds from these frozen, autonomous areas.

Getting Free from the Fear of Freedom

Doreen came to me (Al) on the persistent recommendation of a friend. She had seen a number of counselors over the course of her life and wasn't particularly optimistic that the outcome of our meeting would be any different than what she'd experienced in the past. Nevertheless, she decided she had nothing to lose.

After opening our session in prayer and giving Doreen a quick overview of how the brain works, I inquired about some specific aspects of her phobia. As is usually the case, especially with people who have had extensive therapy, it took a little while for Doreen to understand that I wasn't interested in *why* she was afraid of insects but in *how* she *did* her fear of insects. That is, I wasn't concerned with *why* this happened to her in the past, only in what *she did* in her brain in the present that elicited the remarkable fear she had toward insects. We together discovered that whenever the possibility of coming upon an insect presented itself to Doreen, her brain vividly re-presented her nine-year-old experience of being covered with insects along with the nine-year-old conviction that she was going to die.

Having learned this much, I continued:

> **Al:** Doreen, when you think about the event that occurred so long ago, what do you feel now?
>
> **Doreen:** [*Thinks for a moment about the trauma that occurred to her and thereby triggers the neurochip installed when she was nine.*] I'm terrified!
>
> **Al:** I want you to remember the event again but this time think about how intense this feeling of terror is on a scale of one to ten. *One* means you have no feelings at all, and *ten* means your feelings of terror couldn't be worse.

Doreen's face and entire body immediately became tense and her breathing became more rapid as she remembered this event.

After twenty seconds or so, her eyes opened wide with a look of terror in them. Her face flushed bright pink, and she clenched her fists tightly. These are common physical symptoms of a person experiencing a phobic re-presentation.

Doreen calibrated the intensity of her fear as an off-the-chart twelve! I then helped Doreen exit the Matrix (interrupt the pattern of terror) and reconnect to her mature, thirty-nine-year-old self by asking her about something unrelated to her phobia. In counseling, this is important because the client needs to be on the outside of the Matrix to be a detective of the Matrix. When I saw and heard that Doreen was out of her neurochip of terror, I continued.

I asked Doreen if she'd like to be freed from her fear, to which she responded "of course." When I asked her if she was *sure* she wanted to be free, however, she hesitated. Indeed, the look of terror began to return to her eyes. I could tell the thought of freedom had triggered Doreen's re-presentation. She was pulled back into the Matrix.

This wasn't at all surprising. For most phobic people, the meaning of being set free from their fear is itself terrifying. Though Doreen consciously believed being free from her phobia would enhance her life greatly, her subconscious mind interpreted freedom *from within* her phobia. In her subconscious mind, "being free from the fear of insects" meant she'd have to confront them—or worse than that, she would have to like them—and she didn't want to do that *because they terrified her.* Doreen, like most people with phobias, was caught in a classic Matrix Catch-22.

Not only this, but because Doreen's perspective on insects was frozen in time, she had never integrated a sensible, discriminating approach to insects into her life. Her Matrix neurochip operated with a nine-year-old perspective of terror, concluding that she either must avoid all insects at all costs or she must like the idea of allowing them to crawl on her. From the perspective of this neural-net, therefore, freedom did not mean that Doreen would be free to discriminate between safe and unsafe bugs. It rather meant she'd have to be okay with letting them crawl all over her, which in turn meant that she would be eaten alive.

It was no wonder Doreen at the unconscious emotional level was unsure about getting free. The meaning of being set free for

Doreen had to be addressed before we could proceed further. Once Doreen had exited the Matrix, we continued:

Al: Okay Doreen, I need you to answer a question for me. Are you afraid of heights?

Doreen: What?

Al: Are you afraid of heights?

Doreen: That's an odd question.

Al: I know it seems like an odd question, but are you afraid of heights?

Doreen: No, not at all. I thank the Lord for that.

Al: Would you climb a mountain or hang off the edge of a building without a safety harness to protect you?

Doreen: No! That would be foolish.

Al: But I thought you weren't afraid of heights?

Doreen: That doesn't mean I'm stupid!

Al: I completely agree with you. It would be stupid. And you're certainly not stupid.

Doreen: And this has what to do with my fear?

Al: A lot! Look, Doreen, I have no fear of insects. But that doesn't mean I let them crawl on me. Nor does it mean I'd ever let a tarantula come close to me. Just because I am not afraid of insects doesn't mean I'm stupid. It just means *I have a choice.* I can choose to be amazed at the beauty of certain insects and steer clear of others.

Doreen: Okay, I see what you're getting at.

Al: You need to know that the part of you that is in charge of making sound judgments—like taking ordinary precautions when you're high up—will operate and help you be cautious about insects when you are free. Once you are free, Doreen, *you can* and *will* use the same common sense that you already have in other areas of your life.

Doreen: So you're saying I don't have to like insects? Somehow that thought makes me feel . . . lighter.

AL: No, you don't have to like insects. I don't like most of them myself. And there are a few I would stay away from. But I don't live in fear of them either.

DOREEN: So it's okay if I still want to avoid bugs?

AL: Absolutely, as long as the mature adult part of you is choosing which bugs to avoid instead of having a terrified, nine-year-old neurochip making the choice for you. So, Doreen, do you want to be free?

DOREEN: Yes.

Having collapsed Doreen's fear of freedom, we were ready to begin to tackle the phobia itself.

The Speed and Resiliency of the Brain

AL: Now, how old are you, Doreen?

DOREEN: Thirty-nine.

AL: I want you to remember that. You are *thirty-nine* years old. You're not nine anymore. The nine-year-old didn't know all that you do. She didn't have the resources that you have. She didn't have the learning or experience you have. So Doreen, as the thirty-nine-year-old that you are, do you believe that God wants you to be healed?

DOREEN: Yes, if it's possible.

AL: Doreen, it *is* possible. I know it may sound presumptuous to say this, but when we're through, you're never going to experience that terror again. Your brain is going to physiologically change. We're going to alter the way the meaning of the traumatic event is stored and your re-presentation will be transformed.

DOREEN: When we're through? Like in how many years?

AL: How about today, right now?

DOREEN: [*laughing*] Right, just like that?

    AL: Let me ask you, Doreen, how long did it take for you to learn to be afraid of bugs?

DOREEN: Not long, I suppose.

    AL: It was one event, wasn't it?

DOREEN: Yes.

    AL: And how long did that event take?

DOREEN: It seemed like an eternity, but I suppose it really didn't take very long.

    AL: Think about it as a thirty-nine-year-old, Doreen. The entire episode probably lasted less than a minute, but the actual installation of the messages you internalized about insects took less than a second. The neural-net was created almost instantaneously. And you have suffered with the effects of this up to this point, haven't you?

DOREEN: Yes, it has been very difficult!

    AL: You need to understand that the brain is actually designed to draw conclusions very quickly. This works to our benefit, as God intended, when the beliefs we install are true. But in a fallen world, this efficiency sometimes works against us—as when we draw untrue conclusions about insects. My point is that phobias get installed quickly and *need to be changed quickly.* It is actually difficult to change a phobia slowly.

DOREEN: I see your point. But the phobia got installed because something traumatic happened to me. That's why it was quick. Are you planning on having me go through some kind of de-traumatizing event?

    AL: In a way, yes. But it's not an external event we're talking about. It's a neurological restructuring event.

DOREEN: A *what* event?

    AL: A neurological restructuring event. If you think about it, the event that produces terror in you isn't the *past* event when you were nine years old. *That* event has been behind you for thirty years. What produces fear in you is the neurological event that occurs *in the present* when triggered to do so.

We're going to change *that* neurological event by restructuring the way the neurons fire. After this, the triggers that used to stimulate a distorted, terror-filled re-presentation will instead stimulate an accurate, adult, peace-filled re-presentation.

DOREEN: But we're talking about a memory. You can't just decide to change a memory!

AL: We can't change what happened, but we can change *the meaning* of what happened. For the meaning is simply an electrical-chemical firing in the brain. The pattern of firing—the neural-net—was quickly created when you were nine, and it can be just as quickly restructured when you are thirty-nine.

DOREEN: By a change-in-meaning event?

AL: Yes, exactly. You now run a lie-communicating event in your mind when triggered to do so. We want you to experience a truth-communicating event instead. So, Doreen, are you ready to be set free?

DOREEN: I'm not sure what all this is about . . . but yes, let's do it.

I explained to Doreen that she was now going to enter the "Theater of Life in Christ."[1] This is a concept and an exercise that many have found to be very helpful in the healing process. After explaining the steps of the exercise so Doreen was comfortable with what was going to take place, we continued.

Doreen's Theater of Life in Christ

AL: I'd like you to think about a movie theater. Think about one that is beautiful, warm, and inviting. On the marquee allow yourself to see, "Doreen's Movie Theater of Life in Christ" in big, bright letters. Do you see it?

DOREEN: Yes.

AL: Is it okay if Jesus is in your theater with you?

Doreen: Sure.

    Al: See him walking alongside you into Doreen's Movie Theater of Life in Christ.

Doreen: All right [*laughing slightly*]. I see Jesus with me. It reminds me of Siskel and Ebert in *At the Movies*.

    Al: Great. Once again, Doreen, what is your present age?

I reiterate the point of Doreen's present age and have her repeat it frequently because it's extremely important that this exercise be carried out from the perspective of the adult. One has to be attentive to this because it's very easy to get stuck in the phobic neural-net and have fear dominate one's mind. As we noted above, to be a detective of the Matrix, you have to remain outside it. Or we might say that to wage war within the Matrix, you can't allow yourself to be defined by the Matrix.

Doreen: Why do you keep asking me if I'm thirty-nine?

    Al: Good question, Doreen. The reason it's important that you remember you are thirty-nine is because you are not a little girl anymore. The truth will set you free. You're a thirty-nine-year-old woman sitting next to the one who made you and who loves you so much he died for you. Jesus wants you to be free. Now, Doreen, if you feel anything during this exercise, I need to know. The reason is that you're not in Doreen's Movie Theater of Life in Christ to feel but to *see, hear,* and *learn.* Is it okay if we stop and pray together that the Holy Spirit will help you learn all you need to learn to become the free child of God Jesus died for you to be?

Doreen: Absolutely.

    Al: Holy Spirit, you are called the Counselor for good reason. We are asking you to counsel Doreen during this exercise. Open her eyes to see and her ears to hear truth. Help her to learn what she needs to learn to bring every thought captive to Christ. Help her to know the truth and to be set free by the truth. Heal her and set her free, in Jesus's name we pray. Amen.

DOREEN: Amen.

AL: Okay, Doreen, now remember to tell me if you feel anything during this exercise. Jesus is sitting right next to you, and he wants you to know all that you need to know in order to be completely healed. You're going to create a movie.

DOREEN: *Create* a movie?

AL: Right. This is your brain, so you can have it do whatever you want it to do. Right?

DOREEN: Okay, but I have to say I'm suddenly beginning to feel a little bit nervous.

AL: Thank you for telling me this. Do you know why people feel fear?

DOREEN: Not really; to protect themselves, I guess.

AL: Yes, nervousness, anxiety, and fear are sort of like prophecies about the future, aren't they?

DOREEN: What do you mean?

AL: A part of you is concerned about what is going to happen. It's predicting that this is going to be uncomfortable for you, maybe even scary. It is trying to protect you from being hurt. Does that make sense to you?

DOREEN: Yes.

AL: When you're nervous, it means a part of you is anticipating the future rather than attending to the present. To help anchor you in the present, I want you to look at Jesus sitting next to you. Have the part of you that is nervous speak to Jesus and tell him you are going to trust him for your future. Tell him that for the next few minutes you will completely trust him to protect you. Will you do that?

DOREEN: I did it while you were saying it to me. It's better and I feel calmer.

AL: Excellent. Solidify this commitment by saying to yourself in a loud internal voice, "I will not allow any nervousness or fear because I am trusting Jesus completely right now."

DOREEN: I repeated what you said, and Jesus assured me that it is going to be good.

AL: Now, as you're sitting there with Jesus in Doreen's Movie Theater of Life in Christ, notice the screen in front of you. See the opening credits running down the screen. "Jesus, the Producer and Creator of Life"; "Jesus, the Director of All Transformation"; "Holy Spirit, the Coordinator of Special Effects"; "Holy Spirit, the Great Counselor"; "Holy Spirit, the Organizer of Sounds and Settings"; "Doreen and Jesus, Cooperators for Renewal."

DOREEN: Got it.

AL: And then see the movie title come on. You're watching *The Story of Doreen's Healing.*

DOREEN: This is so incredible. I really like this!

The point of collapsing any feeling of nervousness and running the movie credits is to further anchor a new meaning of "freedom from fear of insects" for Doreen. Until a person has firmly anchored the meaning that change is positive, it is extremely difficult for him or her to move in the direction of transformation.

AL: Are you ready to be free? You and the Holy Spirit will create the movie *The Story of Doreen's Healing.*

DOREEN: Absolutely.

AL: Let's have the movie begin with a pleasant memory of a time *before* the little girl was nine years old and the lie-fear part got in. And let's have the movie end with a pleasant memory of an event that took place *after* she was nine. So think of a pleasant memory before the little girl was nine years old.

DOREEN: [*pauses for a moment*] Okay. I have one. I'm on vacation with my family. I see myself fishing with my dad.

AL: Do you see the little girl up on the screen?

Doreen: Yes.

    Al: How old are you in this memory?

Doreen: I'm six or seven.

    Al: Excellent. I'd like you to see Jesus in the fishing memory, because he was there, right? He's always been with you, and he's always loved you. Can you see him there with the six-year-old little girl?

Doreen: Yes, he is watching me enjoy fishing with my dad. Something interesting just happened.

    Al: What?

Doreen: When I first remembered fishing with my dad, I left out the part where I had to put worms on a hook. But when I introduced Jesus into the memory, I saw myself stringing a worm on the hook. It didn't bother me anymore! It happened automatically.

    Al: Wonderful! It seems that knowing Jesus was with you gave you courage to remember more of the way it actually was. Now get a pleasant memory of a time *after* the nine-year-old's experience.

Doreen: How long after?

    Al: Doesn't matter. Maybe a couple of years.

Doreen: Okay. I'm thinking of my homecoming when I was a senior in high school.

    Al: Tell me about it.

Doreen: I was chosen to be in the royal court. We all wore royal capes, and I was wearing a crown. I wasn't the queen, but I was the homecoming princess. I was really proud. It seems so silly now, but at the time it was huge.

    Al: Sounds like a wonderful memory.

Doreen: [*laughing*] It was my first real date. And it was a cool October night, so there weren't any bugs around!

    Al: Sounds like a really fun time for you. How old are you in this memory?

Doreen: I'm seventeen.

AL: Perfect. See Jesus in this memory as well. Notice how much Jesus is enjoying being with you.

DOREEN: Got it. I really like seeing Jesus in the memories. It seems to bring a new perspective.

AL: You're simply letting your mind re-present the truth, because the truth is that he was there! When we re-present memories *without* him, we're in a way remembering the past incompletely, aren't we?

DOREEN: I never thought about it that way.

AL: Okay, now Doreen, I want you to take a snap shot of yourself in the royal court.

DOREEN: Okay, got it.

AL: Go back into the theater with Jesus. Remember, you're thirty-nine, and Jesus is sitting right next to you. Now it's time to watch the movie of your healing. Notice that you have a remote control in your hand. *You* run the movies in this theater. *You're* in control.

DOREEN: A remote control for a movie in a theater? That's different.

AL: Yes, but this is *your* theater and *your* movie. So *you're* in control. Jesus wants you to have choice and to be free, doesn't he? You can do anything you want in your mind, and the remote control simply re-presents this. I want you to run this movie from the six-year-old fishing memory up to the seventeen-year-old homecoming memory. Notice that Jesus is with you from six to seventeen years old. When you get to the homecoming memory, freeze-frame it on the screen.

DOREEN: This could take a while!

AL: Actually, it won't. Notice that your remote has a super-sonic fast-forward button. You're going to watch this video in super-sonic fast-forward mode while you are sitting next to Jesus. The whole thing will only take a couple of seconds. So, with Jesus by your side, run a super fast-forward movie of your life from the fishing event up to the homecoming event. Make sure you go *through* the nine-year-old's event and up to the homecoming event.

DOREEN: [*giggling*] Okay.

AL: Yes, enjoy it. It's fun. But more importantly, it works. Like I said, the brain is wired to work fast. When you get to the homecoming event, push the *freeze-frame button on your remote, and remember that you're thirty-nine, sitting in a theater with Jesus.*

DOREEN: [*takes a couple of seconds to view her fast-forward movie*] Okay.

AL: Did you *freeze-frame* the last scene? Do you see the seventeen-year-old on the screen at homecoming with Jesus?

DOREEN: Yes.

AL: Fantastic, tell me what you see and how it feels to see you on the screen?

DOREEN: I'm on the football field during half time. I see me looking out at the crowd. I look so young. I'm happy and excited. And Jesus is right beside me, looking proud of me. He seems excited for me as well.

AL: Wonderful. Now, Doreen, *step into* the perspective of your seventeen-year-old self at homecoming. See through your seventeen-year-old eyes and hear the crowd from your seventeen-year-old ears. Smell the October air. Feel the cool breeze on your cheeks. Feel the exhilaration of being on the field. Enjoy the fantastic moment all over again. [*Doreen smiles and takes a deep breath as she associates with this homecoming scene.*] You're enjoying that memory, aren't you?

DOREEN: Oh yes.

AL: Sorry. Can't stay there. I want you to *rewind* the entire movie even faster than you ran the movie forward—*much faster.* You have a super-sonic rewind button on the remote control. Begin with you seeing the stadium through your eyes as a seventeen-year-old and see your history rewind so fast it's a blur of color. It will only take a second. You should end up in the eyes of the six-year-old, experiencing the good feeling of fishing with your dad. Got it?

DOREEN: [*closes her eyes and pauses for a brief moment*] Okay. I am six years old and fishing with my dad again, enjoying the moment.

AL: Tell me what you are experiencing.

DOREEN: I'm just sitting next to my dad, feeling close to him, feeling safe.

AL: And Jesus?

DOREEN: He's on my other side, smiling and enjoying the calm lake.

AL: [*I pattern interrupt Doreen's memory*] Great. Doreen, do you still like to fish? Do you ever take your kids with you?

DOREEN: No, I haven't been able to—because of the bugs.

AL: Well, you will be able to soon. That will be great for you and your family. So tell me, how many children do you have?

My question about Doreen's children was again a *pattern interrupt* to bring Doreen to her present-time consciousness. It's important to exit all association with the memory each time the movie is run backward and go back into the theater seat sitting next to Jesus.

AL: Okay, now back in Doreen's Movie Theater of Life in Christ you go. I want you to do this exact same thing five more times. I want you to begin and end each time knowing that you're a thirty-nine-year-old woman sitting next to Jesus watching a movie. You can have a little popcorn if you want. Are you back in the theater with Jesus?

DOREEN: Yes.

AL: Start by stepping into the seventeen-year-old's eyes and experiencing the joy of the homecoming memory. As soon as you get the good feeling of that seventeen-year-old's moment, zoom back and experience the good feeling of

being a six-year-old fishing with your dad. When you feel the
good feeling of that memory, blank the screen and step back
into your thirty-nine-year-old self sitting next to Jesus again
in the theater watching all of this. Then repeat this four more
times.

Doreen has her eyes closed throughout this process. After
about a minute or so she announces that she's finished. I then
once again perform a pattern interrupt as Doreen and I briefly
talk about what Doreen will do once she leaves my office.

The Nine-Year-Old Meets the Grown-Up

AL: Okay, Doreen, let's see what we've accomplished. I want you
to go back to the nine-year-old memory with the
grasshoppers. Tell me what comes to your mind when you
think of that event. [*Doreen does this for a moment and
giggles.*] It's better, I take it. You don't look like you want to
run from my office the way you did the first time I had you
do this.

DOREEN: Wow, I don't feel anything when I think about that memory.
I know the bug thing happened, but I don't feel anything like
I did before. The focus seems bigger or something. It's funny,
but other things in my life I enjoy flashed before my mind
when I remembered the bug experience.

AL: Tell me a little more about what flashed in your mind.

DOREEN: Well, I suddenly remembered other vacations and fun times I
had with my family. I remembered things I did with my
friends while growing up.

AL: That is so good to hear. It's not uncommon for a person to
have more memories available to them when they become
free of a traumatic incident. Okay, on a one-to-ten scale,
how do you feel when you see you as a little girl with the
grasshoppers on you?

DOREEN: Maybe a three, four at the most. How can that be?

AL: We took a frozen event and connected it to the ongoing dynamic process of life. You helped your brain recognize that you didn't die when you were covered with grasshoppers.

As I'm speaking to Doreen, I look for any bodily signal that might indicate she is looping back into her phobic perspective, especially when I mention her nine-year-old experience. This is another way of testing that the healing has in fact occurred. Throughout the remainder of our time together, however, I see no such signs.

AL: Doreen, your neurochip of fear was activated when any external visual, auditory, olfactory (smell), or touch stimuli were similar to what was present when the grasshopper incident occurred. The neurochip included your nine-year-old's belief that you were going to die a horrible death by being devoured by the insects. What you and the Holy Spirit did just now was help the part of you that was protecting you catch up to the adult's awareness of how it works in reality. This is how we debugged your brain of the neurochip.

DOREEN: That's really interesting.

AL: What you've done is broaden the neurological parameters of your memory so it communicates the truth that this event is simply part of a much larger story—a story that includes some very positive events. You've integrated the nine-year-old with the six-year-old and the seventeen-year-old, and this changes the meaning of the event for the nine-year-old. The neural-net that contained your memory has changed and is now healthy, because it's not isolated from the rest of your brain, so to speak.[2] But the reasons this technique works really don't matter. What matters is that it is very effective in healing the trauma of insects you had as a little girl.

DOREEN: Amen to *that!*

AL: We still have some time left in this session. I'd like to test this change a little further. I want to make sure that you're confident about your healing and that the nine-year-old neural-net is all grown up. So let's go back into Doreen's Movie Theater of Life in Christ. See Jesus sitting next to you.

DOREEN: Got it.

AL: Now, put the scene of the six-year-old up on the screen. Run the movie a bit past the day that you were fishing. See the little girl get up the next day. See her in her bedroom in the house you lived in when you were a little girl. Are you able to do that?

DOREEN: Yes, it's very clear. I remember my room and how it was set up. I had a doll collection, and I can see the different dolls I had when I was six.

AL: Excellent. Now I want you, the thirty-nine-year-old, to step into this scene with Jesus just as the little girl is waking up. The six-year-old sees you and knows she's seeing herself as an adult. Can you do this?

DOREEN: This is a little weird. She seems kind of in awe at seeing me. Her mouth is wide open and she is just amazed.

AL: Meeting your future adult self does that to six-year-olds! Very good. Let's show the little girl some of the scenes of her life that are going to happen to her. Show her some scenes of her future. Begin with her near future and move forward. Show her some of the great friends she's going to make and nice times with the family she's going to experience in the next couple of years. Then, when you get to the nine-year-old scene, keep it going past the insect episode. As a thirty-nine-year-old, show this little girl how she's going to play with friends again and have more good times with her family. Show her that she's going to be a princess at a homecoming when she gets older! And as you do this, Doreen, notice that the little girl doesn't take special notice of the insect episode. It's no big deal to her. She's thinking about how much fun in living she's going to have.

DOREEN: Wow.

AL: Keep your thirty-nine-year-old perspective and show the little girl good things that she'll experience long after the homecoming. Show her how she's going to excel in college and become a very intelligent, successful, and godly woman. Show her how she's going to marry and have some wonderful children. Are you doing this?

DOREEN: Yes. The little girl is just amazed. When I was six years old I was not very attractive, and when I was eleven or twelve I remember wondering if anyone would ever marry me. It's so good for this little girl to see this. She's very excited about her future.

AL: Now I want you to go back to the nine-year-old scene and show the six-year-old girl how adults who are free deal with bugs. The nine-year-old self had been replaying her nightmare every time a bug came along, or when the temperature changed, or when she smelled grass— whenever the possibility of encountering a bug was present. Now you are free and the nine-year-old girl needs to know it. Remember, we are talking about stored information, holographic virtual-reality data that *you have complete control of.* So, Doreen, as a thirty-nine-year-old, freed woman, see the traumatic event when you were nine.

DOREEN: Okay, I see it. I'm showing the six-year-old the nine-year-old's experience.

AL: I want you to now teach the six-year-old little girl that this is a movie *of the past*, and you lived through it. You can do this by fast-forwarding the movie to a week after the nine-year-old's experience with the grasshoppers. Then go two years past the episode, then eight years past to when she'll be a homecoming princess. What you're doing is bringing wisdom to this part of you. You're integrating the nine-year-old's perspective into the rest of your life. You're taking thoughts captive and leading them to truth, as the Bible commands. Are you doing this?

DOREEN: Yes. The little girl understands.

AL: Okay, we're almost done. Go back to the memory of the bugs. I want you as a thirty-nine-year-old to watch this event sitting next to the six-year-old little girl and alongside Jesus. Watch your brother put the grasshoppers down her back. Is it still at a three or four in intensity when you view this?

DOREEN: A three, not a four. I'm seeing this, and I don't like it. But I'm not afraid. I just want to help get those bugs off of her.

AL: You know what Doreen? I was thinking the same thing. How about the six-year-old, Jesus, and you, the thirty-nine-year-old, go and get those grasshoppers off of her. I will be praying for you as you do that. [*Doreen closes her eyes and takes a few minutes to do this exercise. She is radiant when she opens her tear-filled eyes.*]

AL: Doreen, tell me what happened.

DOREEN: At first the nine-year-old was screaming, crying, and frantically flapping her arms because the grasshoppers were all over her back and she couldn't get them off. But then a funny thing happened. I heard the six-year-old say to her, "Look, there aren't very many, and they are only grasshoppers!" She said it like a six-year-old would. It was very matter-of-fact, no big deal. When I looked closely, I could see she was right! There were only about eight or nine grasshoppers on her. Then I held the six-year-old's hand and Jesus took my other hand. Together we got the nine-year-old's attention, and I kept telling her that they were only grasshoppers and that there were only eight of them. I told her she was going to be okay. Right away she started to calm down. I realized that it was the fact that she didn't know what was on her that made her startled imagination go wild. Then the six-year-old picked one of the grasshoppers off of

> her and showed it to the nine-year-old. And—this just floors
> me!—the nine-year-old took one of them off, looked at it,
> and let it go! [*completely breaks into hard sobbing.*]
> **AL:** What is happening, Doreen?
> **DOREEN:** I'm just so relieved!
> **AL:** Praise God! You're free.

I ended my time with Doreen by having her mentally envision the miracle of a caterpillar turning into a butterfly and the incredible complexity of an ant colony. I was testing to make sure the phobia had been conquered and empowering her to actually enjoy and marvel at an aspect of God's creation to which she'd previously been closed. I then had her re-present herself coming upon some ugly bugs—a June bug, a cockroach, and a large spider. I had her calibrate her emotional response when she envisioned these. She responded that she didn't like them—she thought they were "gross"—but that her fear factor was no more than a three. She didn't want them on her, but she didn't feel she had to run away either.

That response, I explained, was completely normal. Most of us would not *want* a cockroach on us. Freedom doesn't mean we'll want to hug the little buggers.

Doreen's Matrix had undergone a revolution. A frozen part of her had been freed. Her life was more congruent with truth, and with God's plan for her life, than it ever had been. And it only required altering an electrical-chemical reaction in her brain that is a centimeter long and a fraction of a second in duration.

No child of the King should be held in lifelong bondage to a momentary, electrical-chemical firing in the brain!

Exercise 8

The Theater of Life in Christ

The goal of this exercise is to empower you to reduce the emotional charge of an incident that has caused you anxiety or fear. It involves ten steps.

Step 1: Recall a memory that is unpleasant, perhaps even traumatic. One way to locate memories that are especially important to work on is to take an attitude, emotion, or behavior you know you need to work on (see exercise 1) and investigate whether any memories are part of your internal strategy for how you do that attitude, emotion, or behavior. For example, several years ago Greg noticed that part of his strategy for doing anger and shame when unable to fix mechanical things was to instantly reexperience fumbling a football in eighth grade that cost his team the game. Become a detective of your mind; find a painful memory to work on.

Step 2: Enter this memory as vividly as possible and then calibrate its emotional intensity on a one-to-ten scale.

Step 3: Now think about a movie theater. Think about one that is beautiful, warm, and inviting. On the marquee allow yourself to see "[Your Name]'s Movie Theater of Life in Christ" in big, bright letters. For some of you the theater and the marquee will be very clear. Others of you will have an awareness that the theater is there but without actually seeing it. There are a host of ways that the movie theater may be re-presented. How you do it is simply how you do it.

Step 4: Invite Jesus to go into your theater with you. Some may find that a part of them resists having Jesus along. If so, ask your soul what this part is and why it resists Jesus's presence. When you discover what it is and why it is resisting Jesus's presence, redo exercise 5 (*Experiencing Jesus*) with this discovery in mind. Whether it is shame, fear of intimacy, or whatever, offer it up to Jesus. Let him express his love for you despite your resistance. Let him convince you that it is safe to include him in every area of your life—and thus into your Theater of Life.

Step 5: When you're comfortable having Jesus along, re-present yourself sitting next to him in your Theater of Life in Christ. The screen comes to life and the two of you view the opening credits. You see:

Jesus, the Producer and Creator of Life
Jesus, the Director of All Transformation
Holy Spirit, the Coordinator of Special Effects
Holy Spirit, the Great Counselor

Holy Spirit, the Organizer of Sounds and Settings
[Your Name] and Jesus, Cooperators for Renewal

You may add a soundtrack to your opening credits if you wish. It's *your* brain and therefore your movie. Finally, see the movie title: *The Story of [Your Name]'s Healing.*

Step 6: As you're sitting in the theater seat, remind yourself of your present age. It's important to remember this throughout the exercise. You are not the age of the person you remember in the memory anymore. Now, on the movie screen view a pleasant memory of a time *before* the time of your painful memory. See yourself in it and enjoy it. This will be the beginning of the movie you are creating. Then remember a pleasant memory that occurred *after* the time of your painful memory. See yourself in it and enjoy it. This memory will be the end of your movie.

Step 7: Sitting next to Jesus in your theater seat while holding a remote control in your hand, run a fast-forward movie of your life beginning with the *first pleasant memory*, running through the painful memory, and ending with the *second pleasant memory*. The entire movie should only take a few seconds, so the scenes between the two pleasant memories will be a fast-forward blur. When you reach the second pleasant memory, at the end associate to (step into) the *you* of this memory and experience it through your own eyes and skin.

Step 8: Enjoy this associated, pleasant memory for a brief moment. Then rewind the entire movie at least twice as fast as you ran it forward. End the rewind with you experiencing your first pleasant memory in an associated way. When you've reached this point, pattern interrupt yourself. Take a moment and think about what you're going to have for lunch tomorrow or something of the sort.

Step 9: Now be back in the theater. Remind yourself you're the age you are and you're sitting next to Jesus. Then repeat steps seven and eight five consecutive times. Remember to pattern interrupt between each memory. Next, see yourself in the early pleasant memory; fast-forward your life through your painful memory up to your second pleasant memory; associate to your second pleasant memory; then rewind the movie twice as fast back to your first pleasant memory. Then be your present self again, sitting next to Jesus watching a blank screen. Then begin the movie again, repeating this four more times.

Step 10: Once you've completed this five times, recall the painful memory and recalibrate its emotional intensity using the same one-to-ten scale. Whatever it was when you started, it should be down to a three or less. If it is not, repeat this entire exercise until it is so.

We encourage you to engage in this exercise—possibly including other elements you saw illustrated in this chapter—for other painful, wounding memories you have. We have consistently found it to be an indispensable tool in equipping people to become detectives of their minds, in taking authority over Matrix neurochips, in being transformed by the renewing of their minds, and in setting the mind free to experience real life in Christ.

9

Finding the Road That Leads Out

Overcoming Depression

TRINITY: Please, Neo. You have to trust me.

NEO: Why?

TRINITY: Because you have been down there, Neo. You know that road. You know exactly where it ends. And I know that's not where you want to be.

———— ❦ ————

I have said these things to you so that my joy may be in you, and that your joy may be complete.

John 15:11 NRSV

Getting Off the Road That Leads Nowhere

Neo had been down that road before. It was a road that led nowhere, for it started and ended within a Matrix that was designed to keep him imprisoned. The only way he could ever get free and discover the joy of being fully alive, of experiencing real love, of having genuine significance, was to trust Trinity and be led out of the Matrix.

On some level, most of us are in the same situation. We find ourselves on familiar roads we know lead nowhere. We habitually engage in the same thoughts, experiences, emotions, and behaviors that invariably lead to the same results. We don't like it, but we don't know what other roads to take. The road we're on may not offer us real life, but at least we're used to it.

There comes a time when you've got to launch out and carve a new path. And as we've seen throughout this work, the place where the new path has to be trod is in the mind. To escape the Matrix, we've got to be willing to give up the familiarity of the Matrix. We've got to be willing to embrace new and initially strange ways of taking control of our minds. We've got to be willing to courageously embrace new re-presentations and interpretations of God, ourselves, and the world.

This chapter is about taking a road out of depression—but we could use any undesirable emotion just as well. For the principles and exercises that apply to depression apply also to anger, lust, jealousy, etc.

Before we adjust the map (experience), however, it will be helpful to examine the territory (truth) because we've got to have a passion for the true territory that outweighs our comfort with our old map. The territory we are concerned with is the territory of God's joyful being and God's joyful will for our lives.

The Joy of the Lord

Though people have traditionally imagined God as a somber and rather irritable being, Scripture frequently depicts God as joyful. True, God is genuinely grieved and angered when people whom he loves bring destruction upon themselves by rejecting him. But it's important we understand that God's fundamental disposition is one of joy.

The Bible describes God as rejoicing, singing, dancing, laughing, throwing parties, and shouting for joy (Isa. 62:5, 19; Jer. 32:41; Zeph. 3:17; Luke 15:3–10). God rejoices whenever others come to participate in his perfect, triune love and joy. In fact, it gave God joy to choose us in Christ from the foundation of the world, to redeem us, and to lavish his love upon us (Eph. 1:4–10). We weren't a nuisance to God. On the contrary, Jesus was willing to endure the nightmare of the cross because of the *joy* of spending eternity with us (Heb. 12:2)!

God wants us to eternally experience his own eternal joy (John 15:11; 17:13). He wants to fill us with "an indescribable and glorious joy" (1 Peter 1:8 NRSV; see also Rom. 15:13). He longs to turn our "wailing into dancing" (Ps. 30:5, 11). Hence, one of the central things the Holy Spirit produces in the life of one who submits to him is joy (Gal. 5:22; 1 Thess. 1:6; see also Acts 13:52). This is why the kingdom of God is described as a kingdom where "righteousness, peace and joy in the Holy Spirit" reign (Rom. 14:17).

People sometimes confuse *joy* with *happiness*. But there is a great difference between these two emotions. Happiness and unhappiness are normal human responses to fortunate and unfortunate circumstances. But the joy God wants us to have can be present whether circumstances are fortunate or not. Joy is a pervasive sense of well-being—even when one is not necessarily happy. Indeed, it can be present even while someone is facing life-threatening persecution (James 1:2).

The Obstacle to Joy

The Matrix feeds off of self-deception, so let's not waste time kidding ourselves; most of us don't experience this joy most of the time. Indeed, many of us not only lack the fullness of God's joy, we experience persistent and sometimes extreme depression. Though we have in fact been placed in Christ and filled with God's joy, something keeps us from experiencing it. What is this "something"?

In some cases, of course, depression may be primarily the result of a chemical imbalance in the brain. Though some misguided Christians have reservations about taking antidepressants, this is really no different from taking medications for any other part of our body. The brain is, after all, *part of our physical body*. If there is a chemical imbalance in a person's brain, therefore, they should have no issue with getting it balanced through medications. Medication helps to place these folks on a level playing field with the rest of us.

The "something" that blocks the joy of the Lord in most of our lives, however, is not a chemical imbalance. It's rather our bondage to the Matrix. The degree to which we have been conformed to the "pattern of this world" is the degree to which we will be prevented from being transformed by the joy of the Lord. For the Matrix is designed and empowered by the Architect whose primary goal is to keep us in bondage to deceptive, debilitating, joy-killing lies.

People usually assume that external circumstances *cause* them to be depressed—or to have any other negative emotion for that matter. We often hear people say that this or that person or event "*made* me" depressed, angry, jealous, etc. This is only partially true, however. External events provide the *occasion* for our emotions, but our emotions are grounded in what *we do* in our brains in response to external events. More specifically, depression is grounded in the mental re-presentations we produce that provide the *interpretation* of external events.

This is why telling people they "ought to" be joyful is never very helpful. Emotions aren't the kind of thing we can directly alter by willpower. What we *can* do is modify our bodily behavior by willpower. So, what often happens when people are told they "ought to" have joy, peace, or love is that they learn how to *act* joyful, peaceful, and loving when they're actually not. This is especially the case when there are social rewards given for people who *appear* joyful, peaceful, or loving (e.g., they are deemed more spiritual). Consequently, the church is full of people trying to crank out a behavioral version of "the fruit of the Spirit" by their willpower. And often this results in people superficially concealing the relative absence of genuine "fruit" in their lives.[1]

We can't *directly* alter emotions with our willpower. But we can *indirectly* affect them by altering the internal re-presentations with which they are associated. Knowing what is true from God's perspective, knowing the authority we have over our brains, and knowing something about how our brains install and modify re-presentations, we can escape emotional bondage within the Matrix.

Mary's Story

Mary was married and had three grown children and four grandchildren. She had been raised by caring parents in a middle-class Christian home with two brothers and four sisters. She had been a committed Christian since she was a young girl. Yet Mary had experienced persistent and severe depression most of her life. She had been in and out of therapy and had tried various medications with little improvement. Nothing excited, motivated, or even interested this chronically tired, cynical, and gloomy woman. On top of all this, Mary was a very anxious person and a ruthless critic of herself. Her life could be summed up in one word: *miserable*.

The first session I (Al) had with Mary was spent teaching her about the nature of the brain and the nature of the Matrix. Mary came to understand that she was designed by God to be in charge of her brain under his lordship, but that Satan's design was to have her brain controlled by the Matrix of this world. In the next session I helped Mary learn how to cooperate with God in order to take her neurochip of depression captive. In the conversation that follows, we will enter her Matrix, learn how she did persistent depression, and see how she was set free from her lifelong bondage.

The World Is a Terrifying Place

AL: Mary, do you feel depressed right now?

MARY: Yes, I am always depressed. That's why I am here.

AL: Okay, Mary, ask your soul, "When did I learn to do this depression?"

MARY: *I* don't *do* depression. Why would I do that? I'm just depressed!

AL: [*We had covered this material, so I responded.*] Remember, Mary, all emotions are associated with re-presentations we *do* in our minds. Though we both know you don't do this intentionally, you do in fact *do* depression. It's a mental behavior you do. What we need to find out is *how* you do depression so we can learn how to help you stop doing depression and start doing joy.

MARY: If you say so, but I really don't understand.

AL: A good way to begin to find out how you *do* depression is to ask your soul when it learned to do depressed. Your neural-net of depression knows everything about how, when, and where to do depression. We simply need to access it. So what I want you to do is think of one of the last times you were really depressed and ask your soul when it learned *how* to *do* depression. Remember, God wants you to assess the substance of your mind and to be a guardian and detective of your thoughts [Prov. 4:23; Heb. 4:12; 11:1]. When you ask your soul, I want you to pay close attention to what occurs in your mind. Your soul will answer you in a few possible ways: you may hear something, see something, feel something, or experience any combination of these. So notice what happens when you ask, "When did I learn how to do depression?"[2]

MARY: [*pauses for a moment*] When I was little.

AL: How did you know that was the answer? Did you hear an internal voice say, "When I was little"?

MARY: No, I saw a picture of me as a little girl.

AL: Okay, very good, Mary. How old are you in this picture that you see?

MARY: I'm not sure. Maybe around nine or ten.

AL: When your soul shows you a picture as an answer to the question, it is letting you know that by that age your belief was installed. There may have been many things leading up to this belief, but the belief was settled by the age of ten. Now, look at that picture of you as a little girl and ask it what happened when you were little that taught you how to do depression.

As Mary asked this question of her soul, she grew noticeably tense, her face turned rather pale, and she began to cry. I could see that Mary had just reentered the Matrix. Whatever Mary experienced as a ten-year-old, she was clearly experiencing it again. And, I strongly suspected, she was experiencing it *as a ten-year-old* (that is, in an "associated" manner).

AL: Okay, Mary, tell me exactly what you saw, heard, and felt just now when you asked your soul that question.

MARY: I was back in my elementary school, and I saw it all over again.

AL: Saw what?

MARY: The film.

AL: Okay, let's slow down. I want to do exactly what you're doing, see exactly what you're seeing, and hear exactly what you're hearing so I can feel (experience) exactly what you're feeling. Are you seeing a snapshot or is it moving like a video?

MARY: [*with her eyes closed*] It's in motion. It's like a video.

AL: Is it in color or black and white?

MARY: Color.

AL: Are you seeing this through your eyes, or are you seeing your body in this video?

MARY: [*pauses*] I don't see my body in the video, so I guess I'm seeing it as I saw it when I was ten, through my own ten-year-old eyes.

AL: Tell me exactly what was there when you were ten.

MARY: [*becoming increasingly agitated*] I am in the school gym, and
I'm sitting on the bleachers. I know the other kids are there,
but I can't see them. It smells like sweat.

AL: You're doing great! Tell me what you're feeling as you're in
this holographic memory.

MARY: I feel fear. I'm confused. I feel so afraid. I'm in shock. I can't
believe it can really be true. This couldn't have happened!
This can't be real!

AL: What can't be real, Mary? What are you seeing?

MARY: [*now extremely emotional*] I am seeing the horrible, awful
movie of the Holocaust. Bodies all over! Children! The
German soldiers did this! How could God let all that evil
happen?

It turns out that in the spring of 1956 all the children in Mary's
class were brought into the school gym to watch a documentary
of the Holocaust. The film included scenes of children being
yanked from their mothers and long lines of adults and children
waiting to be gassed. It included several scenes of piles of dead
bodies. One group had just been gassed, and they had crushed
one another trying to reach a small opening in the top of the
chamber to get air, forming a sort of pyramid. And it included
a grizzly scene of a mass of emaciated bodies being pushed into
a pit with a bulldozer.

As a ten-year-old, Mary did not have the resources to process
this nightmare in a healthy way. She was consequently vicari-
ously traumatized by what she saw. Ever since, whenever the
right trigger was activated—as it was in my office—Mary vir-
tually time-traveled within the Matrix back to this event. She
reexperienced it from the perspective she had at the time. She
was once again sitting on the school bleachers. She could feel
her weight against the benches. She could feel and hear her heart
pounding. She heard all the sounds and words the narrator of
the film said. She could smell the distinct sweaty smell of the
gym. Though she wasn't conscious of it, she was reliving the
horror of what she witnessed as an innocent, naive ten-year-old
little girl. She was caught within the beliefs that were installed
in the Matrix.

This Could Happen to You

AL: Tell me, Mary, what are you thinking as you're sitting in the gym?

MARY: [*She is sobbing and her voice moves from sounding depressed to sounding angry.*] How can people do this to each other? I didn't know these things could happen. It is so horrible. We're in hell! Where is God? Why didn't he stop this? I thought he was supposed to watch over us, protect us, and love us. It's not true. It's not true! We've been lied to. I hear myself screaming inside, trying not to show it.

AL: I know this is hard, Mary. In a little while you'll never have to go through this again. But tell me anything else you're thinking as you're seated in the gym.

MARY: This could happen to me. This could happen to my sisters. This could happen to my mother. If these innocent people were not protected by God, we won't be either. Those poor little children. How can this happen?

AL: What are you feeling, Mary?

MARY: Terror; sadness; confusion; shock; anger!

AL: On a one-to-ten scale, Mary, how high would you rate the intensity of your emotion?

MARY: Ten!

AL: Okay, Mary, is there anything else about this holographic memory that would be good for me to know? I want to do the memory just like you.

MARY: I'm just so afraid that something like this is going to happen to me, my sisters, my mother, my friends.

AL: When you are remembering this memory, how do you know this could happen to you and your family?

MARY: Because it happened to the people on the film! If it happened to them, it could happen to me and my family.

AL: Mary, given what you see, hear, and feel in your mind, and given the little-girl perspective you have of it, I can completely understand how this re-presentation depresses you and makes you anxious. Anyone who saw, heard, and felt what you see, hear, and feel from your ten-year-old perspective would be fearful and depressed.

Christianizing Mary's View of God

After performing a pattern interrupt, I did a check to make sure all aspects of Mary's self were on board with her being healed. As it turns out, a part of her was afraid of letting go of her anxiety and depression because she believed freedom would be followed by tragedy. Being anxious and depressed was her way of staying on guard. We were able to bring this part of Mary on board with our project of getting free by pointing out that even if Mary became joyful and confident, she would still be free to be appropriately cautious of situations that she deemed threatening. It's just that she would also be free from having to see the *entire world* and every situation as threatening. After changing Mary's understanding of "freedom from anxiety" from a negative to a positive concept, we were able to proceed.

> **AL:** Now, Mary, do you believe that God wants you free from your anxiety and depression?
>
> **MARY:** I certainly don't think he's pleased with my life being so sad and depressed.
>
> **AL:** Do you believe that we, working with God, can get you free from your bondage to anxiety and depression?
>
> **MARY:** I want to say yes. And I know I'm supposed to say yes. But please try to understand. I've been counseled, prayed over, and even exorcised so much—well, I'm just a little bit cynical.
>
> **AL:** Fair enough. But what we're going to do in the next few minutes, Mary, is change the Matrix. No one's tried this before with you, have they?
>
> **MARY:** Change the Matrix?
>
> **AL:** We're going to literally restructure your neural-nets, changing the meaning of what you experienced to bring it

> into alignment with truth. We're going to create a truth-communicating event in your brain.
>
> **MARY:** Restructure my neural-nets? Honestly, Al, that sounds a little unrealistic.
>
> **AL:** I completely understand why you would feel that way. You have been practicing the pain for a long time now. But God promises that we can transform and renew our minds. With God, all things are possible, aren't they, Mary?

Mary started to respond but then caught herself. She paused for a moment, and then a tense, angry look came over her face.

> **AL:** I'm thinking we just triggered a neurochip.
>
> **MARY:** Call it what you want. But if everything is possible for God, tell me why he let six million Jews get massacred? Over a million were children and babies!
>
> **AL:** We *have* triggered a neurochip. Okay, let's deal with it.
>
> **MARY:** And how am I supposed to trust that he'll help change me when mothers can't trust him to protect their kids?
>
> **AL:** Mary, share with me a little bit about what you believe regarding free will.

As noted in chapter 5, a person's well-being is intrinsically connected to his or her view of God. Everything hinges on having a re-presentation of God that is trustworthy—that is, Christlike. I thus had to take some time to address Mary's theology. In cases in which people have issues with God allowing evil, we have found that often the best way to proceed is to talk about the issue of free will.

> **MARY:** I think people are free. But God is supposed to be more powerful than our will. So he can stop us whenever he wants. Why didn't he stop the Nazis?
>
> **AL:** If God stopped people from choosing evil, would they be free?

MARY: Maybe not. But it would be worth it.

AL: Are you sure, Mary? Could people be free and therefore capable to love if they weren't also free and therefore capable of acting in unloving ways?

MARY: I suppose not. But at least when young kids are involved, it would be better to take away free will.

AL: At what age do you think God should allow free decisions of others to harm people?

MARY: I have no idea! I'm not God.

AL: That's the point, Mary. You're not God. But when you say it would be better to take free will away, aren't you claiming to know better than God?

MARY: I never thought of it that way, but I suppose I am. It's probably wrong for me to think this way. But it just seems kids should be protected.

AL: We will not change what we don't first doubt. Due to your trauma and Matrix installation, you have been confident for a long time that God did not do his job very well. I'm trying to help you doubt your confidence in this conclusion. Mary, do you believe that Jesus reveals God?

MARY: Of course.

AL: And do you believe that Jesus died for each and every human being?

MARY: Absolutely.

AL: Then you must believe that God has a profound love for each and every human being, including each and every child on earth.

MARY: Okay.

AL: So it can't be that God wanted these adults and children to suffer at the hands of evil people. You wouldn't want this for your children, and God loves his children far more perfectly than you or I.

MARY: You'd think so. But these people *did* suffer. Why?

AL: Rather than letting people's suffering call into question the truth that Jesus reveals God, why not let the revelation of God in Christ call into question your assumption that if people suffer it's because God wants them to? Maybe there's a reason why he can't guarantee that people are always protected.

MARY: He *can't*?

AL: Let's think about it. If there was a cosmic law that kids under the age of twelve couldn't be hurt by a person's free will, how might this affect our overall potential to love?

MARY: I'm not following you.

AL: If no one was free to choose to *harm* kids under the age of twelve, could anyone be free to choose to genuinely *love* kids under the age of twelve?

MARY: Al, I'm not a philosopher, and this is getting pretty philosophical. It just seems God should do something more to protect kids.

AL: This *is* quite philosophical. But here's why it's important, Mary. Much of our philosophy of life is concluded on an unconscious or heart level before we are old enough to reason accurately. What we are doing now is bringing to awareness philosophical and theological decisions that you made due to the trauma you experienced as a little girl. Viewing the Holocaust horror created questions that your ten-year-old mind couldn't effectively answer. It did its best, but as a ten-year-old mind, it had very limited resources with which to work. It therefore drew some terrifying conclusions about God and about life that are inconsistent with the truth that God is revealed in Christ. These theological conclusions are part of the emotional meaning of the re-presentations that get activated under the right conditions, and they keep you depressed and anxious. What we're doing now is calling into question the conclusions of a ten-year-old by thinking as adults about the questions your ten-year-old mind had.

MARY: I see what you're getting at.

AL: Do you agree that you and I don't know enough to judge God for not doing more to protect the people who died in the Holocaust film you watched? Do you see the possibility that he *couldn't* impose the restriction you're asking him to impose without negatively affecting his goal for creation?

MARY: It could be, but I don't like it.

AL: I don't like it either. But if we trust that God looks like Jesus and believe that God is all-loving, allowing this level of freedom *must* be necessary for God's creation to have the potential to love that he desires. God wouldn't just allow children—or anyone—to suffer unless this possibility was necessary for the overall purposes of creation. We *shouldn't* like it when this possibility of evil becomes a reality. But recognizing that this same freedom allows us to love means that we can trust that God looks like Jesus and is all-loving even though the world is sometimes evil.[3]

MARY: Well, I've always believed Jesus revealed God. But maybe I haven't consistently trusted that this is so.

AL: I praise God you believe Jesus reveals God, Mary. But I'm wondering what you *actually experience* in your mind when you think of God. What we consciously believe doesn't affect our lives. It's what we actually see, hear, and sense in our minds that impacts us. So Mary, I want you to become a detective of your mind and honestly investigate what picture of God is dominant in your mind as you wrestle with the questions you were just now raising.

MARY: You want the picture I'm having right now?

AL: Right now. Say, "Soul, listen up. Give me your representation of God's character." Then listen intently and watch intently. Tell me what you hear and see in your mind.

MARY: I know I'm supposed to have a picture of Jesus, right?

AL: There's no "supposed to." We want to know what is *real* to you. Ask your soul this question and observe what it says.

MARY: [*pauses for several moments*] Honestly, I guess I don't think God really cares.

AL: That's information. How do you *do* the thought, "God doesn't care"? Do you hear something? See something? Feel something?

MARY: Okay, this is rather odd. I'm having this image of a sort of W. C. Fields character in my mind. You know, the one who hated kids. I see him looking irritated, folding his arms, and saying in a W. C. Fields sort of voice, "Go away you little buggers, you're bugging me. Go play in traffic or something." It's like he's got more important things to do.

AL: Not too surprising you're having trouble trusting God, is it?

MARY: [*chuckling*] I guess not. I've always felt like a nuisance.

AL: Do you believe this picture is true?

MARY: It feels true.

AL: Of course it *feels* true. It's the re-presentation you have been practicing for some time, so it feels real and comfortable. But do you believe your W. C. Fields re-presentation of God conforms to reality?

MARY: Of course not.

AL: And yet you have it. And this picture—or variations of it—affects all your emotions toward God, yourself, and the world. This explains a lot, doesn't it?

MARY: I didn't know I had it.

AL: What would a true picture of God look like?

MARY: One that looked like Jesus.

AL: The Jesus who died for you on the cross. Exactly.

Mary and I spent the rest of this session replacing her W. C. Fields picture of God with a Jesus picture of God, along the lines discussed in chapter 5. Mary ended up embracing a re-presentation of God whose character could be trusted, even though the world he created is often a threatening place, for her actual re-presentation of God was the one given her by Jesus

Christ. She brought her renegade thought about God captive to Jesus Christ (2 Cor. 10:5).

This alone had a significant effect on Mary's disposition. She experienced God as beautiful and herself as beautifully loved in a way she never had before. It also gave her more courage in the face of a threatening world. People can deal with the painful ambiguity of the world much more effectively when they consistently experience God as loving and experience themselves as loved by God.

This session was over, but we were far from finished. Much work had yet to be done on the faith Mary had about herself and her relationship with God. We were going to adjust this faith by creating a truth-communicating event.

The Faith-Setting Process

In what follows we shall illustrate one powerful technique for affecting our emotions by altering the re-presentational system to which they are associated. We call this technique the "Faith-Setting Process." Faith-setting creates a future-orientated direction for the brain and an expectation of an outcome that the individual will cooperate with God to make happen. It grounds the person in a true re-presentation of himself or herself that pulls the person toward a new and different future.

We began our next session by reviewing some of the theological material we had covered previously. I reminded Mary that we were now going to permanently alter her Matrix by creating a truth-communicating event.

> **AL:** Are you ready?
>
> **MARY:** As ready as I ever could be, I suppose.
>
> **AL:** I want you to remember one of the last times you were depressed. [*Mary nods, almost immediately.*] That was easy, wasn't it? Now, there are a few things that I will ask you to do that are important. Keep in mind, Mary, that your brain is *your* brain and it will do anything you decide you want it to do. Understand?

MARY: Yes.

AL: Okay, the first thing I want you to do is to make sure that the recent picture of you "doing depression" is a still shot. It should have no movement.

MARY: Okay. I have a picture and it's still.

AL: Next, I'd like you to make sure you *see yourself* in this snapshot. I want you to see a re-presentation *of yourself* doing depression. Can you do it that way?

MARY: It just popped right up in my mind. I have a photograph of me depressed . . . from just a few days ago, in fact. I don't like this picture. It's very sad.

AL: I understand. You're doing great, Mary. How many kids did you say you have?

The pattern interrupt is done so that Mary's mind is cleared of the depressed picture before receiving a true, God-given, re-presentation of herself.

AL: Now, Mary, I'd like us to pray and ask God to give you a picture of the *true you*, the *you* that is no longer in bondage. By faith, and with God's help, I want you to get a picture of yourself as you are in Christ, full of joy and peace. God says that he desires you, Mary, to have an abundant life, to fully experience his joy, and to flourish. He wants each of us to experience the fruit of his Spirit: love, joy, peace, patience, kindness, goodness, faithfulness, gentleness, and self-control. All of these aspects of the fruit of the Spirit are *thought processes* that have an emotional component that empowers us to have passion for life [Gal. 5:22–23]. This true *you* is a re-presentation of when you are completely free from depression. As you look at this picture, you don't need to know exactly *how* this *you* was set free. You only need to know that God wants it to be your reality. You just know as you see it that Mary *is* set free. You see it on your face, in your eyes, through your mannerisms. Everything about you manifests a profound peace and contentment. It's the peace and joy of Jesus Christ. I will pray that God gives you the faith you need to move forward. [*As I pray, Mary begins to weep.*] What did God give you, Mary? Tell me what you experienced.

MARY: I saw a picture of a joyful me. I want to be *that* person so bad. But it honestly feels sort of unreal to believe that it could ever be the *true* me.

AL: I understand. This is a very common response. Most people feel this is not real when they do this faith-setting exercise the first time. Doing our faith consciously and purposefully is foreign to most of us and feels kind of fake at first. You have practiced seeing yourself through the mirror of depression for forty-nine years. You're so accustomed to seeing yourself in the mirror of the Matrix that seeing yourself in the mirror of Calvary feels phony. It's important you give yourself permission to see yourself the way God does.

MARY: Even though it feels phony?

AL: Absolutely. Remember, *I'm* not the one claiming this is the true *you*. I didn't give you the picture. *God* says it in his Word, and he just gave you a picture of the true *you* when we asked him. Even though the *depressed you* feels real, on God's authority you know that this joyful picture of you is the *true you*. You need to stand on what God says no matter what the Matrix feels like right now. This is what faith is all about, Mary. Faith is letting God's Word have more credibility to you than your own brain. Faith is holding an expected outcome as a substantial reality in your head and then, eventually, experiencing it as a confident expectation [Heb. 11:1]. So on God's authority, resolve to believe that the *you* who manifests abundant life is the *true you*. Like Job, write it in stone [Job 19:23–27]. Pound a stake in the ground and with willful determination choose to believe it is so. Trust God's Word above every other word or picture your brain might produce. The more you allow yourself to do this faith-setting exercise, the more you practice truth in your mind, the more natural this true picture of yourself will feel.

MARY: It makes sense. And it actually feels very empowering.

AL: Now I'd like you to move ahead in time—what we call "future-pacing." In three months it is going to be Easter. See yourself going to Easter service with your family three months from now. The *you* that you see is the healed *you*, the *you* that has been set free from anxiety and depression, the joyful *you*. As you see this, know that you have been living with this peace and contentment for three months now. Notice how good it feels. Notice how much you're enjoying just being you. See the peace and joy of Jesus Christ being manifested through you.

MARY: You want me to see myself in the future?

AL: Mary, you've been seeing yourself in the future all your life! You've been exercising a fearful Matrix-faith about yourself. But God designed your brain to do whatever you want it to do, and now it's time for you to change this faith to make it agree with God. Faith involves our concrete re-presentations of what we think will be, with the result being a feeling of confidence that it will be so. I'm asking you to have faith that the *you* God knows is true is in fact true. So, can you re-present this true *you* going to Easter service with your family? [*Mary closes her eyes and allows herself to experience this faith-setting process that re-presents her true identity.*] What are you seeing?

MARY: I'm seeing a video of me going to church. For some reason it's more vivid than my previous depressed picture.

AL: You seem moved by it.

MARY: Seeing this makes me want it even more. But it is difficult to believe it could really happen. . . .

AL: You're not used to this. Remind yourself that God said that he will give us anything when we ask for it according to his will [1 John 5:14–15]. Remind yourself that it *is* God's will for you to have abundant, depression-free life. On God's authority, not mine, I assure you that this picture is *already* more true about you than any depressed picture you've ever had of yourself.

MARY: I really want to believe that. But I just don't know.

Mary's repeated reference to the difficulty of believing what God says led me to suspect that some part of her brain was still trying to protect her from being healed. Our brains are exceedingly complex, and our belief systems are multilayered. A person can collapse one neural-net of resistance only to open up other neural-nets of resistance. We previously collapsed Mary's belief that "being free from depression" meant she would be vulnerable to harm. I now discovered that a different part of Mary believed that she didn't deserve to be happy. It turns out that part of Mary's Matrix was the belief that staying miserable was a way of punishing herself for not suffering like some others suffered. On rare occasions when Mary felt an element of joy, this part would make her feel guilty.

We thus spent some time working through this Matrix belief. Mary needed to understand that it wasn't her fault others suffered when she didn't and that it wasn't her job to atone for the suffering of the world. Jesus did this for us on the cross. Mary was eventually able to re-present herself as a person whom God wants to make joyful, even though she, like the rest of us, doesn't deserve it. Once Mary was settled on this issue, we continued:

MARY: How freeing! I never realized part of my brain had taken on Christ's job of rectifying all the suffering of the world.

AL: We never help anyone by assuming guilt for the misery of the world. As you learn to walk in joy, God will show you pockets of suffering he wants you to act on, Mary. He will lead you to alleviate the suffering of others. Obey him, and then put the rest of the suffering of the world on his shoulders. He can handle it. We can't!

MARY: Wow. This feels so much better.

AL: So we agree that God's will for you is to experience his joy
and peace?

MARY: Yes.

AL: You believe that the re-presentation of the healed *you* is
totally consistent with what Scripture says God wants for
you, right? [*Mary nods.*] Okay. Now your role in the healing
process is to simply have faith. You need to hold in your
mind as a concrete re-presentation what God has already
said about you. Will you do that, Mary?

MARY: Absolutely. I will trust that the faith-vision of a joy-filled *me*
attending church with my family is God's will and the true
me.

Smashing Lies with Truth

Having set in stone Mary's faith concerning her true identity,
it was now time to create a truth-communicating event and take
captive the renegade neurochip of her depression.

AL: Now, see the picture of the healed *you* at Easter again.

MARY: Got it.

AL: Okay. Now retrieve the depressed picture of yourself and put
it on the screen of your mind to the left of the picture of the
healed *you*. It's your brain, and you can allow yourself to do
this. Have you got it?

MARY: Yes. But the depressed one is a snapshot and the joyful one
is a video.

AL: Excellent! Tell me other differences you notice between
them.

MARY: Well, the joyful one is very colorful and vivid. The depressed
one is in black and white and is pretty faded. I look really
different in the two pictures. I'm standing different. My head
is up and I look confident in the joyful picture.

AL: Wonderful. Now, here's where things get interesting. We're going to alter the Matrix, just like Neo in *The Matrix*. We're going to smash a lie-communicating event by creating a more powerful truth-communicating event.

MARY: This is that truth-communicating event you were talking about in the first session?

AL: Exactly. See the video of the healed *you* and freeze-frame it. Make it into a still frame, like a snapshot, at the place it feels the very best.

MARY: Got it.

AL: Now take the background out of the still frame so you only see yourself in the picture.

MARY: Why do I have to take the background out?

AL: We want this healed *you* to be a generalization that is true in every situation in which you find yourself, not just when going to church. Your faith is about *you*, not only about *you at church*. Do you have a snapshot of the joyful *you* without the background?

MARY: Yes.

AL: Excellent. Now, take the *old* picture of the *depressed you* and put it in *front* of the true picture of the *healed you*. It's your brain and it will do anything you choose, right now, to do. Did you do that?

MARY: So the bad picture is in front of the good one?

AL: Exactly. Now make the front picture, the depressed one, of glass. You can see the good picture through it.

MARY: So it is kind of a window with my black-and-white photograph on it? Okay.

AL: Make the good picture in the background solid. Make it steel or diamond.

MARY: This *is* getting interesting. Okay, I've done it.

AL: Now see Jesus holding the diamond picture of you healed. Notice the depressed glass picture etching in front of the healed one. [*Mary nods.*] Watch as Jesus takes the diamond picture and smashes it through the glass picture. As you watch, hear the glass of the depressed picture shatter into a million pieces as it falls to the ground. [*It takes Mary only a few seconds to do this.*] Okay, how was it?

MARY: It felt good!

AL: What was good about it?

MARY: It seems a little corny, but I like seeing Jesus and me as a team. I don't feel alone. I know that I can change, and I know where I am heading. It's exciting.

AL: Great! Now this is important. See you and Jesus *sweeping up* the glass and *dumping* it. [*Mary begins to chuckle as she does this.*] Something good is going on. Tell me about it.

MARY: Jesus winked at me with this ear-to-ear smile as he was sweeping up the glass into the dust pan I was holding. Does that sound crazy?

AL: Not at all. That's just like Jesus. He's telling you, "Great job." Do you see or hear anything else?

MARY: I hear Jesus say, "*Finally*, I am so glad you can see the truth!"

AL: Marvelous! Let's do one more thing. I want you to do your faith-setting. Hold up the solid, true, healed picture of *you.* Put it right in front on the screen of your mind.

MARY: Okay.

AL: Enjoy it, Mary. Turn up the color. If there's sound in your re-presentation, turn up the sound.

MARY: All right.

AL: Now this is very important. As you look at the faith picture, thank God with your internal voice for loving and healing you. Tell God in your own words and with an open heart that you commit to having faith that this vision of you is true and that you are committed and willing to do whatever it takes to work with him to see it come to pass.

It's important that you decide to hold this re-presentation as a substantial holographic reality, in full color, and it is important that you express the conviction that it will be so in

your internal voice [Heb. 11:1].[4] Like Jesus says, "According
to your faith let it be done to you" [Matt. 9:29 NRSV].

As I talk, Mary does this with her eyes closed. I instruct Mary
to practice this truth-communicating, faith-setting process three
times a day over the next two weeks. It is important that Mary
practice this process intently in order to set the direction of the
neuro-highway she will be traveling on from this day forward.

Mary's Ongoing Discipleship of the Mind

Mary's altered picture of God, along with her new picture of
herself, brought about a profound change in her life. At the same
time, the Matrix, like the brain it seeks to control, is unfathom-
ably complex. Neural-nets are strung together in incredibly complex and sometimes unexpected ways, and lies can be reinforced
by a multitude of re-presentations. This is why discipleship of
the mind is a day-by-day, minute-by-minute endeavor—for all
of us. One has to be vigilant in employing many different strategies and with detecting hidden, renegade neurochips in order
to continue to maintain and grow in freedom.

In the session following the one illustrated above, we employed the "Mary's Movie Theater of Life in Christ" exercise
(chapter 8) to rescue the ten-year-old Mary from her traumatic
conclusion that life was intolerably terrifying. The adult Mary
could now bring to the young Mary a wisdom the young Mary
did not possess. She came to the conclusion that God would give
her the resources she needs, when she needs them. Mary also
spent a good deal of time resting in Christ (chapter 5) and was
very intentional about running truth-communicating movies of
her identity in Christ throughout the day (chapter 6). She became
disciplined at collapsing her forbidden knowledge of good and
evil and ascribing unsurpassable worth to herself and all other
people throughout the day (chapter 7). She found this discipline
to be particularly powerful in releasing joy, as Mary had previously had a strong accuser and condemner part installed in her
Matrix. And Mary regularly practiced the faith-setting exercise

whenever she caught herself holding untrue re-presentations of herself.

Mary had taken the red pill. She had gotten out of the pod. She had stepped off the familiar but dead-end Matrix road that always led to the same depressing conclusion, and she was learning how to walk on the new neurological road of truth. She was increasingly being transformed by the renewing of her mind and growing in Christlikeness from one degree of glory to another (Rom. 12:2; 2 Cor. 3:17–18). Mary was learning how to wage war within the Matrix and to take every thought, every re-presentation, every neurochip captive to Jesus Christ (2 Cor. 10:3–5). She was becoming the abundantly alive human being God created her, and Jesus saved her, to be.

When Mary went with her family to the Easter service at her church, she had integrated a great deal of the changes for which she had longed. She was becoming the person she had by faith seen in her mind three months earlier. She was manifesting more of the abundant life Jesus Christ died for her to enjoy. She was being set free.

Like Neo at the end of the first *Matrix* movie, Mary was learning how to soar. It is something God wants and empowers every believer to do. For no child of the King should be strapped to the ground by Matrix neurochips. We are empowered to escape the Matrix and set our minds free to experience real life in Jesus Christ.

Exercise 9

Setting Faith for the True You

This exercise helps you collapse the negative Matrix-oriented faith that you are currently doing and install a biblically grounded faith about God's will for your life. The exercise involves seven steps.

Step 1: Form a mental picture that re-presents you doing an emotion, attitude, or behavior that you believe needs to be changed in your life. Once you have it, set it aside and perform a pattern interrupt.

Step 2: Ask God to give you a picture of what you would look like if you manifested the truth of who you are in Christ, freed from this problematic emotion, attitude, or behavior. See yourself being this true *you* in some future situation. Then make it bigger and brighter. If sound is associated with your re-presentation, turn it up. Take a snapshot of this *you* and enjoy the photograph.

Step 3: Delete all background elements of your positive future picture. Then change it to be made out of diamond. Next, place the negative picture in front of this positive picture and make the negative picture out of glass so you can see the positive, diamond picture through it.

Step 4: See Jesus's hands grasping the positive, diamond picture and smashing it through the glass picture. Hear and see it burst into pieces and fall to the ground.

Step 5: Now see Jesus and you step into the picture and sweep up the pieces of broken glass. Dump the pieces into a wastebasket, and see and hear Jesus congratulate you for getting rid of a Matrix lie.

Step 6: Gaze on the positive picture again and make it big and brighter. Thank God that he loves you so much and wants this outcome for your life. With your internal voice, say to your soul that you and the Holy Spirit together will make this positive picture happen.

Step 7: Finally, ask God for his wisdom (James 1:5) to help you discern things in your life that may need to be altered to ensure that this true *you* is manifested. For example, if your problem area is drinking or drug abuse, it would be wise to avoid contexts where alcohol or drugs are present. Ask your soul if there is any part of you that is concerned about changing this strategy. If there is, bring it into the Theater of Life, and discover what it is trying to do for you (see exercise 8). You would be wise as well to invite others you trust to help you attain your goal. Allow God to give you insights into other things that should be included and/or excluded from your life for your faith goal to become experienced reality.

We recommend that you regularly practice this faith-setting exercise: smashing old, deceptive pictures of yourself and replacing them with positive, true re-presentations of yourself. It's also helpful to follow this exercise with the third and fourth steps of exercise 6. See the true *you* in different situations and associate to it. Adjust the submodality distinctions to intensify the truth-communicating event while affirming on God's authority that *this* is the *true you*—the you that was created and saved to experience *real* life in Christ.

Notes

Introduction

1. You need not have seen any of the *Matrix* movies to benefit from this book. You should be advised, however, that throughout this book we use quotes and illustrations from the first *Matrix* movie (*The Matrix*) and, to a much lesser extent, from its first sequel (*The Matrix Reloaded*). We thus recommend viewing at least the original (and by far the best) *Matrix* movie before proceeding. We should in fairness caution you, however, that the movies have foul language and a lot of violence (almost all in a virtual reality world). In our opinion, the benefits of the movie outweigh these deterrents.

Chapter 1: A Splinter in Your Mind

1. George Barna, *Growing True Disciples* (Colorado Springs: Waterbrook, 2001).

2. John Trench, *Galatians*, in Kenneth S. Wuest, *Wuest's Word Studies* (Grand Rapids: Eerdmans, 1983), 1:33.

3. For further discussion of this concept, see Gregory Boyd, *Is God to Blame? Beyond Pat Answers to the Problem of Suffering* (Downers Grove, IL: InterVarsity, 2003); idem, *God at War: The Bible and Spiritual Conflict* (Downers Grove, IL: InterVarsity, 1997).

4. Aside from personal accounts given by Greg and Al, the names and details of all accounts in this book have been altered to preserve the anonymity of the individuals involved. It should also be noted that while all dialogues recorded in this work are actual, they have in most instances been recalled from notes and memory and have been edited for publication.

213

Chapter 2: Interpreting Electrical Signals

1. Those acquainted with developments in neuroscience will know that the analogy of the brain to a computer, used extensively up until the '70s, has been largely abandoned. While computers are information processors, we now know that thought is not primarily conceptual but experiential. When we speak of the brain as our "organic computer" throughout this book, we are referring not to how it *processes information* but to the simple fact that we have to *completely rely on it* for our interaction with the outside world. (While we find this analogy useful, we concede that, as is the case with most analogies, it breaks down at points.)

2. Jeffery Schwartz and S. Begley, *The Mind and the Brain: Neuroplasticity and the Power of Mental Force* (New York: Regan Books, 2002).

3. There is significant debate among neuroscientists about the exact process by which the brain unconsciously draws conclusions about the world. Most now agree that the brain is not merely a blank slate that simply receives input. Rather, neural-nets are formed—and beliefs are arrived at—by a complex interactive process between the brain and the world. A world isn't simply "given" to an infant, in other words. It is "constructed" by the interaction of the infant and others. (See L. Cozolino, *The Neuroscience of Psychotherapy* [New York: W. W. Norton, 2002].) When we speak of neural-nets being "installed," therefore, we do not mean to suggest that the brain is a blank slate, only that the belief embodied in the neural-net was not chosen by the person. It was for the most part chosen *for* him or her. Unless and until we alter this neural-net, we will be influenced by a belief we did not choose.

4. Michael Talbot, *The Holographic Universe* (New York: HarperCollins, 1991). Talbot's book is an exciting and stimulating introduction to the concepts of the holographic brain and the holographic universe. See also the website for Al Larson's Dynamics of Growth Counseling Center, http://www.411growth.com. The holographic model of the brain is one of recent history's most significant advancements in understanding how the brain does the miraculous process of thinking. One of the implications for psychology is the importance of discerning what feels real and is not true from what feels real and is also true.

5. In more technical terms, the frontal lobe region of the brain, where most conscious thought occurs, operates much more slowly than the amygdala, an almond-shaped area of the brain that receives signals of potential perceived danger and sets off a series of reactions that will help protect the person. Our fight-or-flight instinct kicks in before we even think about why we need to fight or flee. We discuss how this reaction occurred in Doreen and how she was delivered from her phobia in chapter 9.

Chapter 3: Entering the Matrix

1. We shall hyphenate the word "re-presentation" throughout this work to emphasize that mental images "make present again" past experiences.

2. A. Korsybski, *Science and Sanity*, 4th ed. (Lakeville, CT: The International Non-Aristotlian Library Publishing Company, 1933). This source is a classic regarding how to use your nervous system more efficiently.

3. G. Lakoff and M. Johnson, *Philosophy in the Flesh* (New York: Basic Books, 1999).

4. Plato, *Philebus* 39c; idem, *Theotatus* 191c, d.

5. Aristotle, *De Interpretatione* 16a; idem, *De Anima* 420b.

6. Noam Chomsky, *Aspects of the Theory of Syntax* (Cambridge, MA: MIT Press, 1965).

7. It might interest some readers to hear a brief (and oversimplistic) neurological explanation for why conceptual information in and of itself can't transform us while experienced events can. To change the way we think, feel, or respond to situations, the relevant network of neurons has to be altered. This involves constructing new synaptic relationships with other neural-nets. This in turn requires that the relevant neural-net as well as the new neural-nets fire together. (Donald Hebb coined the classic phrase, "neurons that fire together wire together." Donald O. Hebb, *The Organization of Behavior* [New York: John Wiley & Sons, 1949].) Simultaneous activation creates new synaptic connections. Conceptual information *about* an event does not activate the relevant neural-nets, but emotion-laden experiences do. In the terms of this book, old Matrix-oriented neural-nets are rerouted only when they are circuited into a broader context—one that reflects truth rather than the myopic, distorted perspective of the original Matrix neural-net. Hence, we shall see in part 2 that we rely on "truth-communicating *events*" to bring about transformation. We enter the Matrix of a neural-net—have the person *experience* the lie—and then integrate it into a broader, truer perspective (including the perspective of God's Word).

8. Technically speaking, when triggers activate fight-or-flight responses, such as in Doreen's case, the emotion *precedes* the re-presentation, for the amygdala that releases the chemical cocktail into the body that produces emotion operates faster than the neocortex that re-presents images associated with the emotion. Both the emotional charge and the re-presentations that are associated to them occur much faster than the conscious mind ordinarily detects. As we shall see in part 2, in order for transformation to occur, we must become aware of our re-presentations in order to consciously alter them. This changes the meaning of our re-presentations and collapses the triggers that evoked the fight-or-flight response.

9. R. Bandler, *Using Your Brain for a Change* (Moab, UT: Real People Press, 1985).

Chapter 4: Waging War within the Matrix

1. For more information on the concept of Cooperating with God for a Change®, see Al Larson's website, http://www.411growth.com.

2. For dissenting perspectives, see J. Schwartz and S. Begley, *The Mind and the Brain*. Twice the New Testament distinguishes between our "soul" (*psyche*, in Greek, meaning "mind," "soul," or "heart") and our "spirit," which denotes our innermost being (1 Thess. 5:23; Heb. 4:12).

3. While Scripture distinguishes between the *body*, *soul*, and *spirit*, it consistently depicts humans as unitary wholes, not composite beings made up of two (or three) separable substances. We thus think it best to conceptualize the threefold distinction as three *aspects* or *dimensions* of the human self rather

than three separable substances. The center of the self, the innermost being, is identified as *spirit*. The thoughts and emotions—our personality—are identified as *soul*. And our physical body, including our physical brain, is *body*.

Chapter 5: Opening Up Our Eyes

1. For more on this subject, see Gregory A. Boyd, *Repenting of Religion: Turning from Judgment to the Love of God* (Grand Rapids: Baker Books, 2004).

2. For more on this subject, see Gregory A. Boyd, *Seeing Is Believing: Experiencing Jesus through Imaginative Prayer* (Grand Rapids: Baker Books, 2004).

3. For a fuller exploration of this form of prayer, see Boyd, *Seeing Is Believing*.

Chapter 6: Taking the Red Pill

1. For further discussion, see Boyd, *Repenting of Religion*.

2. The neurological explanation for why vividly experienced events have such a lasting impact has to do with the fact that when we are emotionally aroused, positively or negatively, our awareness of what is going on around us is greatly heightened. Emotion networks, which are subcortical, signal cortical areas to pay attention to stimuli that are relevant to the positive or negative state we are experiencing, as well as activating cortico-hippocampal memory-formation systems to remember this for future benefit. (The cortico-hippocampal system is the primary system involved in establishing explicit memory, or conscious memory.) The emotional component of the experience serves to create and strengthen neural connections. Among other things, when emotion activates arousal, the hormone/neurotransmitter norepinephrine, a chemical that is now known to increase memory retention, is released in the brain. This is why, for example, Doreen could be pulled back into the Matrix of her bug phobia by the mere smell of grass—for her brain experienced this smell in her hyperalert emotional state and remembered it as significant.

3. In counseling hundreds of men (and a few women) on pornography addiction over the last twenty years, I have been amazed at how similar—even down to certain details—the God-given "faith" about pornography tends to be. Mark's re-presentation of God's view of pornography was rather typical.

Chapter 7: The Kiss of Trinity

1. For a fuller discussion on the Tree of the Knowledge of Good and Evil and how it blocks love, see Boyd, *Repenting of Religion*.

Chapter 8: Matrix Revolutions

1. For more information on the "Theater of Life in Christ™," see http://www.411growth.com. This technique is adapted from the "fast phobic cure" used in Neuro-Linguistic Programming (NLP). See Bandler, *Using Your Brain for a Change*; and J. O'Connor and J. Seymour, *Introducing Neuro-Linguistic Programming: Psychological Skills for Understanding and Influencing People*, rev. ed (San Francisco: Thorsons, 1990).

2. The more technical neurological explanation for why this exercise works is that it creates new synaptic relationships between the phobic neural-net and other neural-nets. It thereby integrates the myopic, distorted perspective of the phobic neural-net with other neural-nets, thereby destroying the emotional meaning of the phobic neural-net. The principle in play is that "neurons that fire together wire together" (Hebb, *The Organization of Behavior*). Conceptual information itself could not do this for the simple reason that conceptual information doesn't activate the relevant neural-nets. We must experience the relevant neural-nets' re-presentations in order to integrate them. As we've said, one must *enter* the Matrix (without being defined by it) and bend its rules in order to escape the Matrix. For Doreen, the primary relevant neural-nets/re-presentations were her phobic nine-year-old experience and her six-year-old and seventeen-year-old pleasant memories. The exercises that follow strengthen the new, broadened neurological circuitry and expand it farther.

Chapter 9: Finding the Road That Leads Out

1. Since people are psychosomatic wholes, altering bodily behavior sometimes affects one's disposition. For example, putting a smile on your face by sheer willpower can sometimes make one feel happier. But doing so at the expense of addressing the underlying causes of one's depression is harmful. One may feel a bit happier by acting happy, but one will never discover the genuine joy of the Spirit in this fashion. (See Boyd, *Seeing Is Believing*, chapters 1–4 in which the "try harder" approach to issues is probed more thoroughly.)

2. When we address our souls, we are assuming the position of what we call the "I" of the soul. The I of the soul is the wisdom position and the connecting place between spirit (our innermost being) and soul (our thoughts and emotions). To become a detective of the mind one must have an active "I." The "I" of the soul is the conscious guardian and detective of the innermost thoughts within the soul. For more information on the "I" of the soul, see http://www.411growth.com.

3. For a more in-depth discussion along these lines, see Boyd, *Is God to Blame?*

4. On the nature of faith and the "faith-setting process," see http://www.411 growth.com.

Bibliography

This biography includes not only works cited in *Escaping the Matrix* but also other works that might be of interest to those who want to do further reading on the way the brain works. Brief comments on works are offered where we feel it might be helpful to readers.

Aristotle. *De Anima*
———. *De Interpretatione.*
———. *De Memoria.*

Bandler, R. *Using Your Brain for a Change.* Moab, UT: Real People Press, 1985. A classic NLP text by one of the founders of the movement.

Barna, G. *Growing True Disciples.* Colorado Springs: Waterbrook, 2001.

Baum, K. and R. Trubo. *The Mental Edge: Maximize Your Sports Potential with the Mind/Body Connection.* New York: Perigee, 1999.

Boyd, G. *Is God to Blame? Moving Beyond Pat Answers to the Problem of Suffering.* Downers Grove, IL: InterVarsity, 2003. Argues that the mystery of suffering attaches to the infinite complexity of the world, not to the character or purposes of God. Helps preserve a Christ-centered mental picture of God in an ambiguous world.

———. *Repenting of Religion: Turning from Judgment to the Love of God.* Grand Rapids: Baker Books, 2004. Fleshes out the connection between love, judgment, and the knowledge of good and evil.

———. *Seeing Is Believing: Experiencing Jesus through Imaginative Prayer.* Grand Rapids: Baker Books, 2004. Discusses the biblical and ecclesiastical background of cataphatic (imaginative) prayer and then offers practical help in practicing it.

Churchland, P. *Scientific Realism and the Plasticity of Mind.* Cambridge: Cambridge University Press, 1979. A classic work defending the view that an exhaustive account of the brain's activity can be given without appealing to mental images (a view sometimes called "eliminativism"). The view doesn't deny that people experience mental images, only that these images play any *causal* role in thought.

Churchland, P. S. and T. J. Sejnowski. *The Computational Brain*. Cambridge, MA: MIT Press, 1992. Presents and defends the connectionist-computational model of the brain.

Cozolino, L. *The Neuroscience of Psychotherapy*. New York: W. W. Norton, 2002. An excellent work on how recent discoveries in the field of neuroscience can aid psychotherapists in their clinical work with clients by using approaches that are designed according to how the brain functions.

Damasio, A. *The Feeling of What Happens*. New York: Harcourt, 1999. Best-selling author/neuroscientist Antonio Damasio explores human emotion, its grounding in the body, and how this contributes to human consciousness.

Danziger, K. "The History of Introspection Reconsidered." *Journal of the History of the Behavioral Sciences* 16 (1980): 241–62. Succinct and helpful history of thoughts on the nature of ideas and how this has impacted behavioral sciences.

Ellis, R. D. *Questioning Consciousness: The Interplay of Imagery, Cognition and Emotion in the Human Brain*. Amsterdam: John Benjamins, 1995. A comprehensive refutation of all past and present criticisms of the view that the mind thinks with images as well as a comprehensive presentation of evidence from a number of fields for the centrality of imagination in thought. Some of Ellis's own constructive proposals, however, are disputable.

Esrock, E. J. *The Reader's Eye: Visual Imaging as Reader Response*. Baltimore: Johns Hopkins University Press, 1994. Demonstrates the interconnection between imagination and reader interpretation.

Hall, M., and B. Bodenhamer. "Neuro-Semantics," http://www.Neurosemantics .com/index.html. Introduces readers to *neuro-semantics*, a brilliant and thorough integration of insights and techniques from NLP and other cognitive therapies with a Christian worldview.

Hebb, D. O. *The Organization of Behavior*. New York: John Wiley & Sons, 1949. A classic book that was far ahead of its time in thinking about the neurological wiring of the brain and how it determines emotions and behavior.

Kosslyn, S. M. *Ghosts in the Mind's Machine*. New York: W. W. Norton, 1983. Fascinating and groundbreaking defense of the pictorialist view of images (namely, that images are like pictures—"quasi-pictorial").

———. *Image and Brain: The Resolution of the Imagery Debate*. Cambridge, MA: MIT Press, 1994. Defends the analog side of the analog-proposition debate on a neurological basis—arguing that visual, auditory, and kinesthetic images are not reducible to a more fundamental, computational language.

Lakoff, G. and M. Johnson. *Philosophy in the Flesh*. New York: Basic Books, 1999. A truly outstanding work showing how recent advances in cognitive sciences reveal that all thought is "embodied" and thus that all abstract thought is metaphorically rooted in concrete experience. Lakoff and Johnson then show, ingeniously and controversially, the implications these insights have for classic philosophical problems.

Larson, A. http://www.411growth.com. Website for Al Larson's Dynamics of Growth Counseling, Consulting, and Training Center. Larson utilizes insights from Scripture, NLP, and other cognitive therapies within a context of a Christian worldview.

LeDoux, J. *The Emotional Brain*. New York: Touchstone, 1996. A masterful, neuroscientific exploration of human emotion, from its role and function in life to its neurological underpinnings.

———. *Synaptic Self*. New York: Penguin Books, 2002. An excellent and thorough introduction to neuroscientific thinking on how the brain works and how our synaptic connections develop over time and make us who we are.

McMahon, C. E. "Images as Motives and Motivators: A Historical Perspective." *American Journal of Psychology* 86 (1973): 465–90. Suggests that motivation is experienced as an emotional component of images of a desired outcome.

Neisser, U. "A Paradigm Shift in Psychology." *Science* 176 (1972): 628–30. Summarizes arguments that led to the academic return to the classic "folk psychology" view that humans think with images.

Newton, N. "Experience and Imagery." *Southern Journal of Philosophy* 21 (1982): 475–87. Strong argument that nonvisual (e.g., auditory, kinesthetic) images are central to thought.

O'Conner, J. and J. Seymour. *Introducing Neuro-Linguistic Programming: Psychological Skills for Understanding and Influencing People*. Rev. ed. San Francisco: Thorsons, 1990. One of the best introductions to NLP.

Paivio, A. *Imagery and Verbal Processes*. Reprint, Hillsdale, NJ: Erlbaum, 1979. Forceful case that memory consists of visual and auditory images, providing much empirical evidence on the mnemonic effects of imagery. This work played an important role in restoring mental imagery as a scientifically respectable topic after decades of neglect due to the influence of positivism and behaviorism.

———. *Mental Representations: A Dual Coding Approach*. New York: Oxford University Press, 1986. A definitive statement of the "dual coding" theory of cognitive processes (namely, the view that thought is coded in visual and auditory images).

Plato. *Philebus*.

———. *Theatatus*.

Pylyshyn, Z. W. "Mental Imagery: In Search of a Theory." *Behavioral and Brain Sciences* 25 (2002): 157–237. Continues to defend the propositional pole of the analog/propositional debate, despite Kosslyn's claim to victory for the analog (pictorialist) side.

Roszak, T. *The Cult of Information*. Berkeley: University of California Press, 1994. A refutation of the notion that we think primarily with conceptual information.

St. Francis de Sales. *Introduction to the Devout Life*. Translated by John Ryan. New York: Doubleday, 1955. Emphasizes the importance of imagination in a person's devotional life.

St. Ignatius. *Spiritual Exercises*. Translated by Joseph Tetlow. New York: Crossroad, 1992. The classic sixteenth century work on cataphatic spirituality.

Schwartz, J. and S. Begley. *The Mind and the Brain: Neuroplasticity and the Power of Mental Force*. New York: Regan Books, 2002. Perhaps the best recent defense of the view that humans have a soul that transcends their neurological activity and that can significantly shape their neurological activity.

Shepard, R. N. and L. A. Cooper. *Mental Images and Their Transformations*. Cambridge, MA: MIT Press, 1982. Explores the brain's capacity to manipulate and transform mental images to gain information and alter behavior.

Shepard, R. N. and J. Metzler. "Mental Rotation of Three-Dimensional Objects." *Science* 171 (1971): 701–3. Renowned experiment demonstrating how we replicate our experience of the world in our images.

Siegel, D. J. *The Developing Mind*. New York: Guilford, 1999. An overview of how the human mind forms from birth on via interpersonal interaction. It serves as an excellent introduction to the basic systems and functions of the mind.

Thomas, N. J. T. "Experience and Theory as Determinants of Attitudes Toward Mental Representation: The Case of Knight Dunlap and the Vanishing Images of J. B. Watson." *American Journal of Psychology* 102 (1989): 395–412.

———. "mental imagery, philosophical issues about," s.v., in *Encyclopedia of Cognitive Science*. Vol. 3. ed. L. Nadel. London: Nature Publishing/Macmillan, 2003. Excellent, succinct overview of the history of thought about the nature and role of mental images.

Titchener, E. B. *Lectures on the Experimental Psychology of the Thought-Processes*. New York: Macmillan, 1909. A defense of the classical view of thought as images against the rising "imageless thought" perspective of W. Wundt, J. B. Watson, and Dunlap at the turn of the twentieth century.

Tye, M. *The Imagery Debate*. Cambridge, MA: MIT Press, 1991. Perhaps the best overview of the debate between pictorialists and descriptionalists in the image debate. Tye himself makes a powerful case for a mediating position.

Yates, F. A. *The Art of Memory*. London: Routledge and Kegan Paul, 1966. A classic work on mnemonic uses of imagery from ancient times to the Renaissance. Shows the importance of mental imagery in Western thought. Was instrumental in the return to mental imagery as an academically respectful topic in the '70s.

Gregory A. Boyd is founder and senior pastor of Woodland Hills Church in St. Paul, Minnesota, and founder and president of Christus Victor Ministries. He was professor of theology from 1986 to 2002 at Bethel Seminary in St. Paul. Boyd is a graduate of Princeton Theological Seminary (Ph.D.), Yale University Divinity School (M.Div.), and the University of Minnesota (BA). He is a national and international conference speaker and has authored thirteen previous books, including *Is God to Blame?*, *Seeing Is Believing*, *Repenting of Religion*, and the award-winning *Letters from a Skeptic*. He is cofounder of Theosynergistic Neuro-Transformation® (TNT). Boyd and his wife, Shelley, live in St. Paul and have three children.

Al Larson is the president of Dynamics of Growth, Inc., which provides counseling to families and individuals as well as consultation for business professionals. He is the founder and developer of Theosynergistic Neuro-Transformation® (TNT) and of a dynamic new concept in Christian counseling called "Cooperating with God for a Change®." Larson holds an MA in psychology from Liberty University and a doctorate in clinical pastoral counseling from the Minnesota Graduate School of Theology. He is a nationally board certified counselor and is a member of the North American Psychologist Association. He is also a supervising therapist with the American Academy of Clinical Family Therapists. Al and his wife, Sue, live in St. Paul; they have two children and seven grandchildren.

Also by **Gregory A. Boyd**

Gregory A. Boyd

seeing is *believing*

Experience Jesus
through
Imaginative Prayer

0-8010-6502-X • $12.99p

Break out of spiritual performance into a liberating relationship with Christ through the power of imaginative prayer.

"[Boyd] makes a powerfully persuasive argument for the use of imaginative prayer by Christians, then outlines a method for beginning the practice."
—*Publishers Weekly,*
starred review

"This is one of the most comprehensive books ever written on the subject. It will not only clear away much misunderstanding, but inspire many to experience the healing freedom and deeper relationship with Jesus that comes through imaginative prayer."
—David A. Seamands, author of *Healing for Damaged Emotions*

"So many books on spirituality offer 'pie in the sky' solutions, but not *Seeing Is Believing.* I love the way Boyd explains and helps us to live out the true identity that we have in Jesus Christ."
—Robert E. Webber, author of *The Younger Evangelicals*

AVAILABLE AT YOUR LOCAL BOOKSTORE